CW01651070

A Perfect World in

Ribbon embroidery & stumpwork

5-MAR-07
I do hope you enjoy this book.
Have fun!
Love
Di van Niekerk
www.dicraft.co.za

PROUDLY SOUTH AFRICAN®

A Perfect World in Ribbon embroidery & stumpwork

Di van Niekerk

METZ PRESS

If you have bought the book you are allowed to reproduce the designs in this book for your own personal use without prior permission from the publisher or author. Copying of the designs for any commercial teaching or retail purposes whatsoever is not allowed under any circumstances.

This book is for André, Ryan and Brandon, my family and sanctuary. And for Verde, a very gifted artist.

Every effort has been made by the author and the publisher to ensure that the information and instructions in this publication are correct. The results cannot be guaranteed and no warranties are given. No liability can be accepted for any injury, loss or damage suffered.

Published by Metz Press
1 Cameronians Avenue
Welgemoed, 7530 South Africa

First published in 2006

Publisher Wilsia Metz
Design and lay-out Lindie Metz
Illustrations André Plant
Photographer Ivan Naudé
Reproduction Color/Fuzion
Printed and bound in China by WKT Company
ISBN 1-919992-48-0

Contents

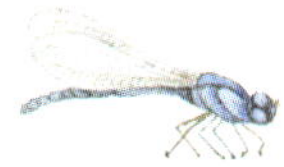

Introduction

This book is packed with new ideas and techniques in ribbon embroidery and stumpwork for both the beginner and the more advanced embroiderer. There are instructions for over 60 elements ranging from beautiful plants to tiny creatures, shown step by step, with detailed photographs to guide you. What's more, the tiny creatures and flowers are perfect for quiltmaking, scrapbooking, or for appliqué on clothing and handbags along with other crafts listed on page 147. Each element in every panel is presented with a list of requirements and stitches for easy reference.

Embroider the complete sampler or select one panel for smaller projects. Or choose a single element from a panel (a beautiful moth or a bunch of English bluebells, for instance) and add these to your own design, whatever craft you are engaged in! Hints are included throughout and these will help avoid any snags along the way.

I have also included new ideas for insect wings and flowers, along with other short-cut suggestions that will save you a great deal of time and effort. Please bear in mind that the photographs are of exceptional quality and are enlarged for easy reference. The texture of the ribbon is actually silky smooth and the stitches are smaller than those shown in the pictures.

The design for this book was painted in watercolour by Verde, one of South Africa's most gifted artists. The design and the A3 measurements are included at the back of the book for your own personal use. Please note that you are only allowed to copy the design for personal use, from the book you have bought. See page 13 (printing the appliqué shapes) for information on how to transfer the design onto fabric.

For your convenience, the full-colour design, printed on top quality pure cotton, is available from selected retail outlets worldwide and from our website www.dicraft.co.za. Please be aware that there are cheap and nasty counterfeit fabric prints out there, and to steer clear of sub-standard materials, do contact us for a list of accredited outlets.

For the best result, it is much easier to embroider the design on a full-colour print as the artist's meticulous detail on the print guides you as you stitch – a similar concept to working on a tapestry canvas.

For needle crafters wishing to choose their own colours and background, however, a line-drawing of the design has been included on page 151.

The small shapes (wings, petals, leaves and others) included in the various panels are the right size for an A3 design and measurements are included with full-colour design on page 150. If you wish to make a larger or smaller panel, flower or creature, use the shapes in the panel as a guideline and trace directly from your enlarged or reduced pattern. This way they will fit your own creation.

I do hope your masterpiece becomes a much loved family heirloom. Have fun!

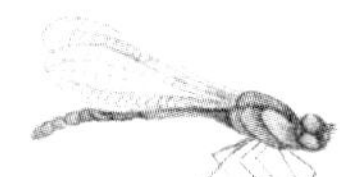

What you need

I have listed specific requirements for every panel of the sampler. Should you decide to embroider any individual creatures or flowers, such as the honeybee or cosmos, you will find the requirements in that panel's list.

General requirements

General necessities are a small pair of embroidery scissors with sharp points for cutting out the shapes, and an old pair of scissors, wire cutters or nail clippers for cutting the wires. You may want to use tweezers for bending the wire. You will need a 15 cm (6 in) and a 20 cm (8 in) hoop for most of the smaller shapes that are embroidered separately, also some pins, a pincushion, needle grabber or small round piece of soft rubber to help pull the needle through, HB, 2B, 3B and 4B pencils, blue water-soluble pen and masking tape for taping the wires at the back of the work.

Fray Stop or any good anti-fray liquid is used – check that it dries clear before using it on your embroidery. You need water-soluble fabric (a thin plastic fabric that dissolves in water,) medium-weight iron-on interfacing, an off-cut of white organza and soft cotton or polycotton fabric, a small piece of white or green felt, a selection of beads available from most haberdashery stores and stamens and wire available from cake decorating stores.

For highlighting you need some white and yellow metallic thread available from sewing-machine shops, a water-soluble glue stick – similar to those used for school projects – and some toy filling or shredded wadding/batting. Most of these items are easily obtainable but if you cannot find anything, contact us for a list of suppliers in your area.

You will need daylight or good light with a comfortable chair and work table as it is preferable to have all your ribbon and threads in front of you. Hoop stands are available from needlecraft shops that hold the hoop so that both your hands are free to work.

Clean hands are essential, so keep some wet wipes or a damp cloth close by and a new resolve to spend more time each week creating your masterpiece! Embroidery is probably the best therapy there is for time-out from our hectic lifestyles.

Needles

For ribbon embroidery, it is essential that the needle makes a large enough hole in the fabric so that the ribbon is pulled through gently without snagging or damaging the silk. The ribbon spreads evenly to form a soft, open stitch, instead of being all scrunched up after being pulled through too small a hole. The eye of the needle must also be large enough for the ribbon to lie flat once threaded.

You need only four types of needles for the projects in this book and I have listed the sizes required under each section. Buy a mixed pack, so all the sizes are in one pack. The lower the number, the thicker the needle.

- Chenille no 18/24 (mixed pack). This is a thick needle with a sharp point and a large eye. The no 16 chenille needle-pack is used for the wider ribbon and for making holes for the wired stumpwork shapes.
- Crewel/embroidery no 5/10 (mixed pack). This is a sharp, fine needle with a long, large eye. The finest no 10 needle is ideal for beading.
- Straw/milliner's needle no 3/9 (mixed pack). This is a long, sharp needle with small eye which is no wider than the shaft. This is the only needle to use for bullion knots. The wraps slip off the needle easily as the eye is not too wide. The finest no 9 needle is ideal for beading.
- Tapestry needle no 13. This is a thick needle with a blunt point. The no 13 needle is ideal for making loop stitches.

Ribbons and threads

The ribbons used in this book are from my own hand-painted range of silk and organza ribbons, available from needlecraft suppliers worldwide. I find that the handpainted, multicoloured or variegated ribbons are the best to use, as they help to create a more authentic picture consistent with the look of real flowers and leaves.

Plain or solid silk ribbons can also be used in combination with these if you already have them, but I find that the design tends to be flat and lacks atmosphere and depth if only solid colours are used.

I used mainly Chameleon and Rajmahal Art. Silk threads. Feel free to use whatever thread you like, but try to choose the specified colours to match the design.

Ribbon embroidery

Ribbon needs to be worked flat for most of the stitches. Use only short lengths of ribbon (30 cm or 12 in), as longer pieces will fray if pulled through the fabric too often. It is also difficult to work with ribbon that is too long and the quality of the stitch is affected. Thread the needle and pierce the end of the ribbon that has just been threaded as shown below. Pull the long tail to tighten the knot.

To start, leave a small tail at the back and, as you make your first or second stitch, pierce the tail to attach it to the fabric. You can also anchor the tail with embroidery thread or knot the ribbons as you would a thread. The texture of the design is busy enough to hide the bulkiness of the knot.

To finish, leave a tail 1–2 cm (½ in) long at the back of the work and secure the tail to the fabric with embroidery thread or catch the tail when you start your next stitch. You can also weave the ribbon in and out of adjacent stitches at the back.

When you work, use your left thumb (or your right thumb if you're left handed) to hold the ribbon flat as you pull it through to the back. Only let go once the stitch is almost completed. This prevents the ribbon from twisting.

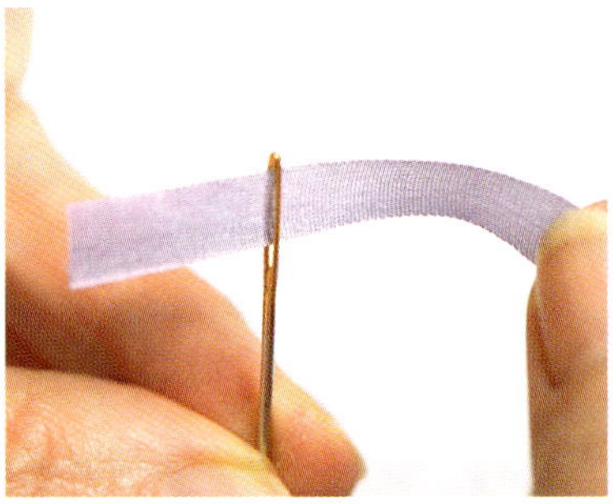

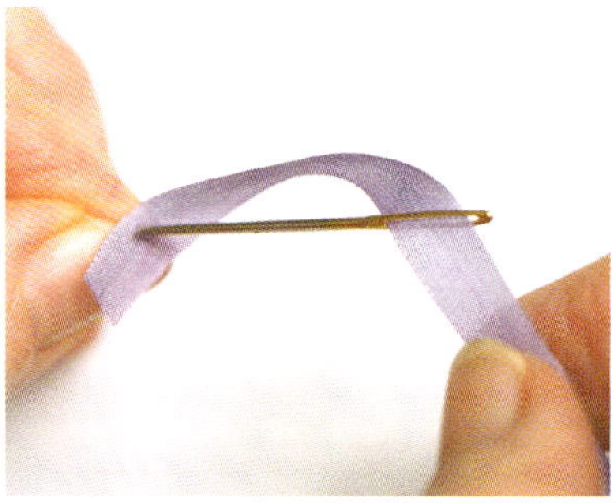

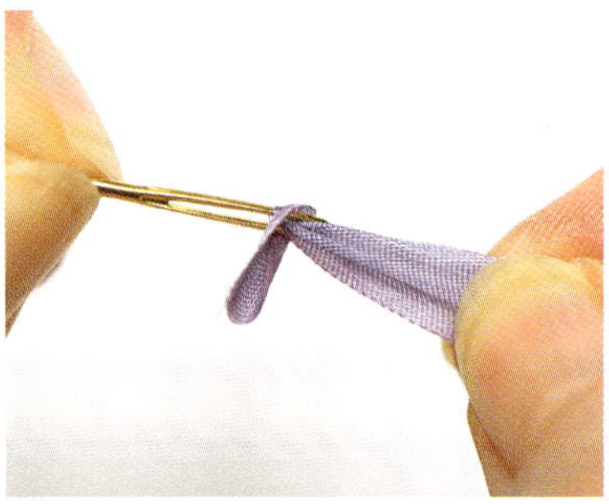

Work with a gentle tension and keep the stitches loose and unfolded. Allow the ribbon to spread easily to its full width on the fabric before starting the next stitch. If you pull a stitch too tight in error, don't be deterred; simply make another stitch on top of it. This will add texture to the design.

Stumpwork

Stumpwork is a raised form of embroidery that originated in Europe in the 14th century and was given this name by the Victorians. Stumpwork is an uncomplicated technique, easy to learn and allows for beautiful three-dimensional effects in a design. Simple stitches are used to create beautiful flowers and insects with padding, wiring, beading and water-soluble fabric. With stumpwork, shapes are embroidered on a separate piece of fabric, and then cut out to be attached to the main design.

Stumpwork leaves

Various techniques for stumpwork leaves are shown step by step under the different panels in this book. Wire is used along the edge of some leaves that are bent into shape. Other leaves do not require wire along the edge. The leaf is formed on a separate piece of fabric in long and short buttonhole stitch. Cut out the shape and then attach it to the design. This technique is useful for shapes that do not need to be bent into shape.

Barbola stumpwork

Barbola is an ancient Tibetan form of stumpwork where layers of fabric are used to create raised embroidered shapes. This technique is used for the strelitzia in panel 6 (see page 59). No wiring is used along the edge and a fabric stiffener such as an anti-fray agent or glue paste is used to stiffen and strengthen the embroidered shapes before they are attached to the main embroidery. Barbola is a surprisingly easy form of stumpwork and saves a great deal of time as no wires have to be attached and covered.

Stumpwork petals

There are a number of methods to choose from when creating flower petals.

Using separate organza petals is a lovely way to create open cup-like flowers like poppies, old roses and camellias. For flowers such as penstemon, the outer trumpet shape is made separately and attached on top of organza ribbon to form a raised flower. To create round flowers such as ericas, the petals are formed over a bead.

Interesting petals are made using a new ribbon appliqué

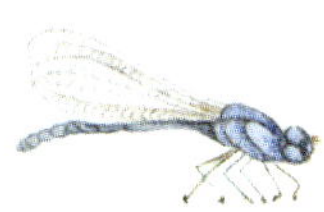

technique. The petals are made separately on interfacing that is ironed to silk or organza ribbon, cut out and then applied to the design – a form of free-standing appliqué. The shapes are easy to make, even for inexperienced needle crafters, and save a huge amount of time and effort that would normally be spent on filling shapes with embroidery stitches. The free standing appliqué shapes add an interesting texture and combine well with ribbon embroidery and stumpwork.

Flower centres and cones

The centre of a flower always makes it more realistic and determines a good finish. There are many ways to form the centres and often the flower does not look like a flower at all until the centre is completed.

Changing the centre also allows you to change the flower. For instance, the poppy with its distinctive centre in Panel 17 (see page 138), can be changed in an instant to an old fashioned rose by simply adding a circle of golden yellow French knots. Flower centres can be flat, fat and rounded or have stamens. The cone-like flower centres of the leucadendrons have a special appeal, while the French knots used for the raised centres of the sunflowers, perfectly resemble 'the real thing'.

Insect wings

Stumpwork insects add a beautiful touch to any project. I have included ideas in each panel on how to use these charming creatures for scrapbooking, card making, trinket boxes, quilt making and other crafts.

Insect wings are made in several ways. Some wings are edged with wire and filled with embroidery stitches, while other wings are made with a wire edge on sheer organza. An interesting variation, introduced for the first time, is free-standing ribbon appliqué wings. This is a great method to use for quick and easy insect wings and the organza ribbon used has a lovely shine, resulting in a delicate, lifelike finish.

Appliqué Perse

Broderie Perse (the French for Persian embroidery) or *appliqué Perse* evolved in the 1700s when shapes printed on expensive chintz fabric were cut out and appliquéd to quilts and clothing. This way one piece of chintz went a long way! The cut-out shapes were stitched onto the background with blanket stitch around the raw edges, or in the case of laundered articles, a small seam was turned inwards before the shape was stitched to the background with slip stitch.

Free-standing appliqué shapes are used in Panel 14. The chameleon in Panel 4 can be appliquéd as well. The appliqué shapes are easy to make and save a lot of time and effort if you do not fill the shapes with embroidery stitches. They add an interesting texture and combine well with ribbon embroidery and stumpwork.

Printing the appliqué shapes

For your convenience, pre-printed shapes are available from www.dicraft.co.za, or ask us for details of your nearest stockist.

To print the shapes onto fabric yourself, you can use any of three methods, depending on your printer. Before printing the shapes, scan them in and reverse them, and ensure they are the correct size for the A3 design.

Using transfer sheets with an inkjet printer Purchase transfer sheets (T-shirt transfers) from any office supply store or craft outlet. Never use fabric or transfer paper in a laser printer. Laser printers work with heat and you will ruin your printer. Scan the images and increase colour and density on your computer. Follow the manufacturer's instructions and print these onto the transfer paper. Iron onto smooth, white, pre-shrunk cotton fabric – the smoother the fabric, the better the result. You may need to experiment with different brands of transfer paper to find a finish that is not too plastic once printed.

Printing the images onto fabric Use specially treated fabric sheets that are made for most inkjet and bubble-jet printers and are available from quilting outlets. Scan the images and increase colour and density on your computer. Print the images onto this fabric following the manufacturer's instructions.

Transfer the images using the solvent method You can only use this method if you have a laser printer. Scan the image and increase colour and density on your computer.

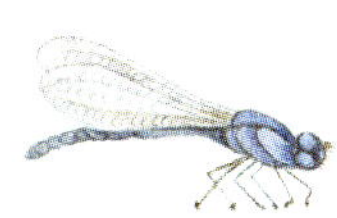

Print on 100 gsm coated paper (with coated paper the toner sits on top of the paper, ensuring a better transfer). Work with disposable gloves in a well ventilated area. Tape the print right side down onto smooth, white, pre-shrunk cotton fabric, stretched over a hard surface. Soak a ball of cotton wool or surgical gauze in liquid thinners (although some people prefer acetone) and dab onto the wrong side of the paper, wetting the image. Using the back of a teaspoon, rub the wet image, applying pressure, working in a circular motion. Carefully lift one corner to check if the image has been transferred to the fabric. Allow to dry and rinse in tepid water to remove the solvent. Press with an iron to heat set and remove the creases.

If you do not have a scanner and/or printer, have colour copies made at any copy shop. Show them the copyright permission in the book (for personal use only) and they should not have a problem doing it for you (on coated paper). Then follow the solvent method.

Before you start

This book is designed for you to make use of the watercolour to print onto cloth, or the black line-drawing to trace off. Both images have been included (see pages 150 and 151) along with the measurements of the completed image.

Prepare the design

I recommend that you work on a cloth printed in full colour as discussed in the introduction. Alternatively, trace the line drawing on page 151 onto your background of choice. Choose a suitable shade of white, cream, pale green, blue, rust or dusty pink fabric, taking into account that a tracing may be difficult to see on darker shades. Fabrics such as pure cotton, or cotton blends, linen or linen blends and Dupioni silk (also known as Douppioni or Dupion silk) are a good choice. The fabric block is 60 x 60 cm (about 24 x 24 inches) square, so it fits well in a 45,7 cm or 18 inch quilting hoop. The fabric needs to be a medium weight that is strong enough to hold all the stitches, but with a loose enough weave for the ribbon to pass through without being damaged. Ensure your chosen background fabric is preshrunk and free of creases by dry-cleaning or washing and ironing according to the manufacturer's instructions.

Should you wish to choose your own colours, enlarge the black line-drawing on page 151 to the size specified and trace onto your chosen fabric. Lay the prepared fabric on top of the enlarged drawing and pin or tape in place.

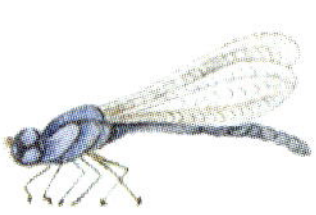

Ensure the fabric is smooth and stretched quite tight over the pattern. Use a sharp HB or 2B pencil and carefully trace the design. A light box is handy if the chosen fabric is too dark to see the lines clearly. Use a ruler to draw the straight lines and draw lightly and neatly, sharpening the pencil frequently.

Cut an extra layer of soft white muslin, lawn, or polyester silk as backing fabric to stabilize and support the embroidered fabric. Ensure the backing fabric is the same size as the embroidery block.

Preparing the hoop

You will need a 45,7 cm or 18 inch quilting hoop for the A3 design. This way most of the embroidery is done on the hoop, apart from the corners that are completed once the embroidery is removed from the hoop. Prepare your quilting hoop by binding both the inner and outer rings with strips of white bias binding or fabric. Wind a full circle and overlap the starting point by about 3 cm (1 in). Secure in place with needle and thread. This binding gives the hoop a tighter grip and protects the embroidery cloth.

Keeping your work clean

To keep your embroidery clean, use the window method as follows: Cut a block of inexpensive white fabric, the same size as your embroidery cloth. Place the hoop on top of this fabric and draw a circle 5 cm (2 inches) inside the edge of the hoop, ensuring that the circle is smaller than the hoop. Cut out the circle to make a window and place this layer on top of the embroidery cloth. This "window" fabric prevents the edges of the embroidery from getting dirty.

Inserting the work in a hoop

Place the embroidery cloth (right side up) on top of the backing fabric. Lay the window fabric on top of the embroidery cloth. Insert the three layers in the quilting hoop. Stretch all the layers as taut as a drum. Ensure that the backing fabric is wrinkle free and tighten the hoop. Roll up the corners of the fabric and pin or tack out of the way. This prevents you from stitching the corners onto the back of the work by mistake.

Hint: *Remember to tighten the layers in the hoop every now and then as you work, so the background does not pucker. Pull all the layers gently at each corner and tighten the hoop.*

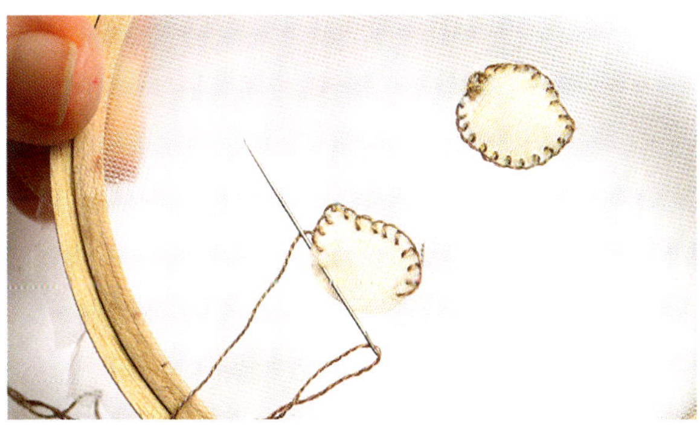

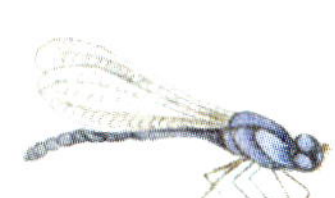

PANEL ONE

Tulbaghia

Clivia

Oxalis

Dragonfly

Tulbaghia violacea

Common names: wild garlic, society garlic, pink agapanthus, wildeknoffel

A fast-growing bulb reaching about 40 to 70 cm in height, with lilac, violet, lavender, pink flowers. Beautiful smooth, slender grey/green leaves that are eaten like chives and used in soups, salads and stews. The plant has medicinal value and is said to have anti-bacterial properties. Makes a good mosquito and flea repellent when rubbed on exposed skin. The flowers are strongly scented and give off an aromatic garlic odour as do the leaves that smell strongly of garlic when crushed. Makes a beautiful container plant and looks good in rockeries, helping to get rid of moles. Likes full sun, (won't grow in the shade) and dry soil conditions. Tulbaghia violacea *attracts birds, butterflies, bees, moths and other insects to the garden and flowers for long periods in midsummer to early autumn.*

Hint: *Embroider this interesting flower to add that special touch to a beautiful scrapbook page, or for card-making. Embroider on a cotton background, stretch and mount before gluing to the page or card. Embroider directly on handbag or jersey or background of a trinket box.*

REQUIREMENTS

2 x 3-mm necklace beads and 1 x 5-mm bead in lavender, pale pink, green or clear
White-ipped stamens from a cake decorating shop

CHAMELEON THREADS

Pure silk: Green Apples no 40, Black Berry no 8, Wisteria no 95, Rustic Brick no 66
Stranded cotton: Baked Earth no 7
Use 1 strand of thread unless otherwise specified

DI VAN NIEKERK'S RIBBONS

Silk: 7-mm no 76, 4-mm no 35 and 74

STITCHES

Detached buttonhole stitch, stem stitch, straight/stab stitch, straight stitch – twisted, grab stitch, ribbon stitch, seeding stitch

NEEDLES

No 8 or no 9 crewel for two strands of thread, no 9 or no 10 crewel for one strand of thread
No 16 chenille needle to form hole in centre of the wild garlic; no 18 or 20 chenille for the 7-mm ribbon and no 20 or no 22 for the 4-mm ribbon

Start with the long stem. Use two strands of the green thread and make one long straight stitch from the base (on the ground) to the centre of the flower cluster to form the foundation stitch of the detached buttonhole. The stitch is about 6,5 cm (2½ in) in length. Pull the thread taut. Start from the base again and make about 9 to 12 long, straight stitches close together and overlapping one another. Use the same thread (two strands) and insert the needle under the entire cluster of straight stitches. Form closely packed detached buttonhole stitches around all of the straight stitches with the buttonhole edge on the left or the right to create the detached stem of the flower. Note the needle is only taken to the back of the work if you need to rethread, or once the stem has been covered and you need to end off the thread.

Change to the Black Berry thread and form the seven slender pedicels holding each flower and bud in stem stitch for the curved stalks and straight/stab stitch for the straight ones.

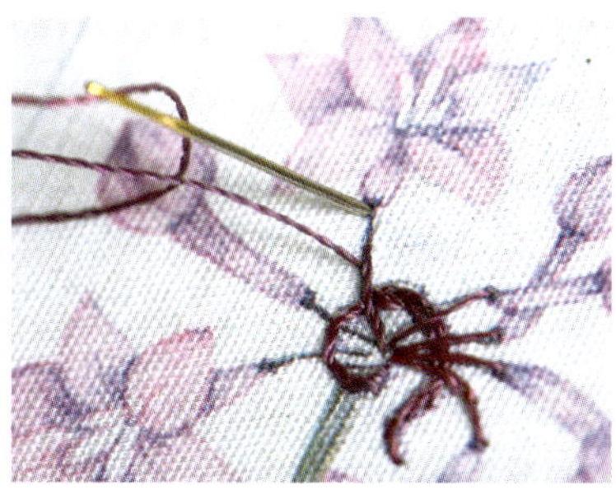

Thread up with the 4-mm silk ribbon and form the leaves in straight stitch, twisting the ribbon for the long leaf on the left of the stalk. I added another shorter straight stitch on top for a thicker texture. Use the brown

thread and wind it under and over the twisted leaf for an interesting effect. The very thin leaves on the far left are made with the 2-mm green ribbon and twisted straight stitch.

Make the closed flower buds. Secure the 5-mm bead to the background on top of the left bud with 3 or 4 stitches in 2 strands of wisteria thread. Repeat with the 3-mm beads for the smaller round buds on the right. Thread the size 18 chenille needle with the 7-mm lavender ribbon. Cover the bead in ribbon stitch; insert the needle at an angle under the bead, so the ribbon fits snugly around the bead. Repeat two or three times, so the bead is well covered.

Change to the 4-mm pink ribbon and add a few pink straight stitches on top. Use the same ribbon and a grab stitch at the base of the bud to form a rounded calyx.

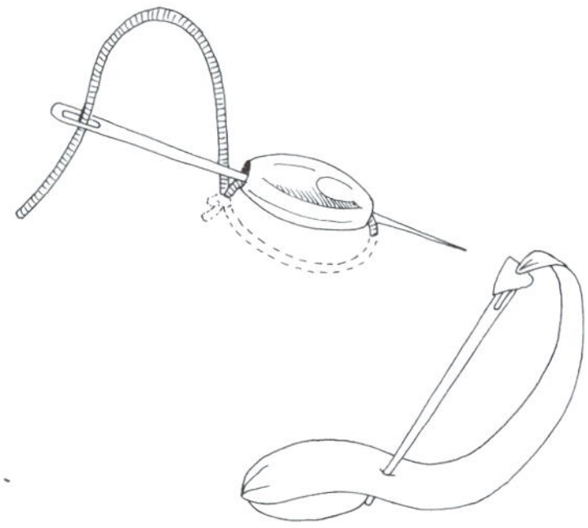

Thread up with the 7-mm ribbon again and **form the tubular flowers** in ribbon stitch, working from the centre outwards. Leave a small opening in the centre so the stamens will fit later. Change to the pink ribbon and make a few pink ribbon stitches on top of the blue ones for an attractive display of colour. Thread up with the Black Berry thread and make 2 or 3 tiny stab stitches along the tip of each ribbon petal to anchor it to the fabric, ensuring that the stamens will not pull the petals out of shape when inserted.

Complete by adding **the stamens**. Use the no 16 chenille needle (or the sharp tip of the small embroidery scissors) to make a hole in the centre of the flower. Take care not to pull the petals out of shape. (If this does happen, simply make another stitch on top later.) Fold the stamen in half and thread the folded section through the eye of the needle. Take the needle to the back, working with a gentle tension. Hold onto the stamen tips on the right side so they are not pulled through by mistake. Cut another stamen in half and pull through gently as before so there are 3 stamens. Gently pull the tips of the stamens back

to the front until you are happy with the length. Use the Wisteria thread and small stab stitches to attach the stamens in the centre of the flower. Bend the stems of the stamens at the back and secure with stab stitch. Cut off excess stems. Repeat for the other flowers and finally add a pink petal in ribbon stitch on top of the flower on the right.

The ground

Use the brown thread and seeding stitch or tiny stab stitches between the pink oxalis on the ground. (Work the ground before embroidering the pink oxalis as set out on page 20.)

Seeding is small stab stitches made close together, in different directions, at random intervals to form an interesting texture or to create shadows in a design.

Clivia miniata

Common names: bush lily, St John's lily, fire lily, boslelie.

From the Amaryllis family and endemic to South Africa, growing wild in shady forests of Kwazulu-Natal, the Eastern Cape, Swaziland and Mpumalanga. First sent to England from Kwazulu-Natal in the 1800s and now cultivated all over the world especially in Japan, China, Australia and Europe. This much-loved, beautiful evergreen perennial has trumpet-like flowers ranging from deep reds and orange to salmon and yellow, growing from thick stalks between shiny dark green strap-like leaves. Clivias like dappled shade, will burn in direct sun, and are sensitive to frost. They don't require frequent watering or lots of natural light, and this is why they are such rewarding house plants. They take three to five years to flower, flower in spring to summer and like to be left undisturbed for many years. Wonderful cut flowers.

REQUIREMENTS

4 x 3 or 4-mm green bicone Swarovski® Crystal beads from beading shops
White-tipped stamens from a cake decorating shop

CHAMELEON THREADS

Pure silk: Tropical Green no 3
Use 1 strand of thread unless otherwise specified

DI VAN NIEKERK'S RIBBONS

Silk: 7-mm no 47, 2-mm no 118

STITCHES

Straight/stab stitch, straight stitch – twisted, grab stitch, ribbon stitch, French knot

NEEDLES

Use the no 8 or no 9 crewel for two strands of thread, no 9 or no 10 crewel for one strand of thread and beading
Use the no 16 chenille needle for the hole of the stamens, no 18 or no 20 chenille for the 7-mm ribbon and no 22 or no 24 for the 2-mm ribbon

Outline the stems using the 2-mm green ribbon and twisted straight stitch. Keep the tension quite loose, so the ribbon will form a nice curve once stitched in place with thread. Stitch over the flowers as these will be added on top later. Thread up with the green thread and use tiny stab stitches here and there to coax the ribbon stem into shape.

Form the apricot-coloured petals starting with the flower closest to the dragonfly. Thread up with the 7-mm apricot ribbon and form three ribbon stitches, first the centre petal and overlap it on both sides. Repeat for the remaining flowers.

Change to the green thread and form a grab stitch at the tip of each petal to anchor it to the design and to form a sharp green point. Add a few straight/stab stitches to the tip of each ribbon petal for further shading.

Use the same green thread and attach a crystal bead at the base of four flowers. Use four or five stitches to secure the bead. Form French knots at the base of the remaining two flowers in the same green thread, wrapping around the needle three times.

Fold one stamen in half and insert into the top flower as shown in the step-by-step instructions for Tulbaghia (wild garlic) on page 18. Secure in place with the green thread. Repeat for the other flowers.

Oxalis purpurea

Common name: sorrel, suring

*Largely native to South America and Southern Africa. Low-growing annual or perennial herbs, found in sub-tropical or tropical parts of the world, although some occur in mild temperatures. They like sun to partial shade and are good container plants, as they bloom continuously. It is said there more than 700 oxalis species world-wide, well known for their fragile, vibrant flowers with five petals. Most oxalis have oxalis acid in their genetic make-up (*oxalis *comes from the Greek* oxis, *which means* acid*) and some are used for salads. Ranging in colour from pink to magenta, red, yellow and white, they are mainly grown as ornamental plants. They have clover-like leaves that close up at night and are tolerant of dry conditions.*

REQUIREMENTS
Mill Hill frosted glass beads no 62044 White tipped stamens from a cake decorating shop
CHAMELEON THREADS
Pure silk: Egg Yolk no 28, Cyclamen no 22 Forest Shade no 33 Use 1 strand of thread unless otherwise specified
DI VAN NIEKERK'S RIBBONS
Silk: 7-mm no 43, 2-mm no 36
STITCHES
Stem stitch, straight/stab stitch, ribbon stitch, French knot, lazy daisy/detached chain stitch
NEEDLES
Use the no 9 or no 10 crewel for one strand of thread and beading Use the no 18 or no 20 chenille for the 7-mm ribbon and no 22 or no 24 for the 2-mm ribbon

Hint: *Use the water-soluble fabric technique to make beautiful individual flowers for scrapbook pages or card making, and for embellishing quilts, jerseys or attaching to a dress panel or pocket. Instead of embroidering the flowers directly on the design as shown below, insert a block of water-soluble fabric in a 15 cm (6 in) hoop. Embroider each flower as shown here on the fabric, and cut out the shapes, leaving an edge of 0,5 cm (¼ in). Place the flowers in a bowl of water for a few minutes to dissolve the fabric. Remove, place on a soft towel and allow to dry. Attach to your page with acid-free glue or use a matching yellow thread to secure to jerseys or clothing. See the Panel 11, Cosmos petals (page 95) for more information on working with water-soluble fabric.*

Form the pink oxalis flowers. Thread up with the pink 7-mm ribbon and use a ribbon stitch for each petal. The buds are formed in the same stitch. Thread up with the yellow thread and attach a bead with four anchor stitches in the centre of each open flower. Add a few tiny yellow French knots (2 wraps) alongside each bead. Change to the pink thread and add a few pink French knots as before to form the shadows in the centre.

Form the stems in the green thread using stem or straight stitch. Change to the green 2-mm silk ribbon and form the leaves in lazy daisy/detached chain stitch.

The green calyx on the tiny bud is made in ribbon stitch.

Dragonfly

Order Odonata, suborder Anisoptera

Dragonflies are predatory insects named for their large jaws that are used to catch other insects in mid-flight. They have four beautiful, iridescent wings, and, like all insects, six legs and three body parts: a head, a thorax and an abdomen. They have been around for more than 300 million years. They are essential to mankind as they prey on mosquitoes and flies. To do so they have large eyes with very good eyesight and are strong fliers, occasionally reaching speeds of 50 km per hour.

Hint: *Use the water-soluble fabric technique to make a detached dragonfly for scrapbook pages or for card-making. Instead of embroidering the dragonfly directly on the design as shown here, insert a block of water-soluble fabric in a 15 or 20 cm (6 or 8 in) hoop. Trace and embroider the head, thorax, abdomen and wings as shown here and cut out the shapes leaving an edge of 5 mm (¼ in). Place in a bowl of water for a few minutes to dissolve the fabric. Remove, allow to dry on a soft towel, assemble as shown here and attach to your page with acid-free glue. Draw in the legs with a black fine-liner pen. Alternatively, embroider the dragonfly directly on the fabric as shown here, to embellish quilts, jerseys or onto a dress panel or pocket.*

REQUIREMENTS

Mill Hill beads no 42041
20 x 20 cm each white organza and water-soluble fabric
#30 wire
Fray Stop or anti-fray agent

CHAMELEON THREADS

Pure silk: Peacock no 103
Scottish Heather no 68
Use 1 strand of thread unless otherwise specified

RAJMAHAL ART SILK

Lagerfeld Ink no 25 or Charcoal no 29

STITCHES

Satin stitch, padded satin stitch, pistil stitch, overcast stitch, couching, buttonhole stitch, running stitch, stab/straight stitch, stem stitch, French knot, split stitch

NEEDLES

Use the no 9 or no 10 crewel for the silk threads and the no 10 for beading

Wing shapes

Use a sharp 2B or 3B pencil and trace the two wing shapes above right in the centre of the white organza block. Draw in the veins on each wing as neatly as possible. Place the organza, pencil side up, on top of the water-soluble fabric block.

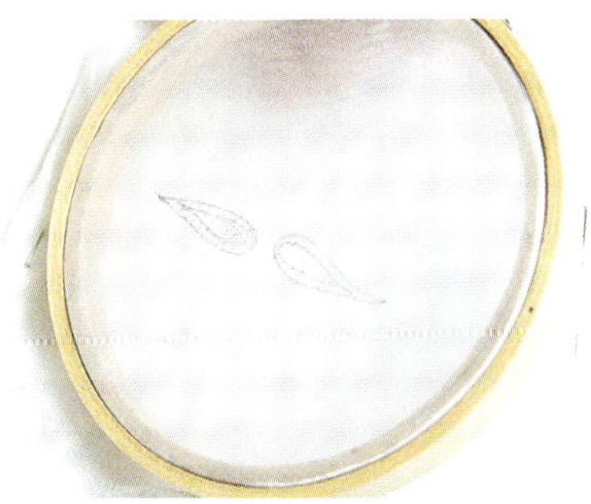

The water-soluble fabric forms a stabilizer for the organza. Insert both layers in the 15 cm (6 in) hoop. Being careful not to tear the water-soluble fabric, gently pull both layers taut and tighten the hoop. Roll or cut the corners away, so they don't hinder you as you work.

Use the #30 wire for the wings. First strip the plastic coating off the wire by holding the wire on a towel or dishcloth. Use the outer blunt edge of the old pair of scissors and run the scissors over the wire to strip the coating. This way the wire is finer and not too thick for the delicate wings.

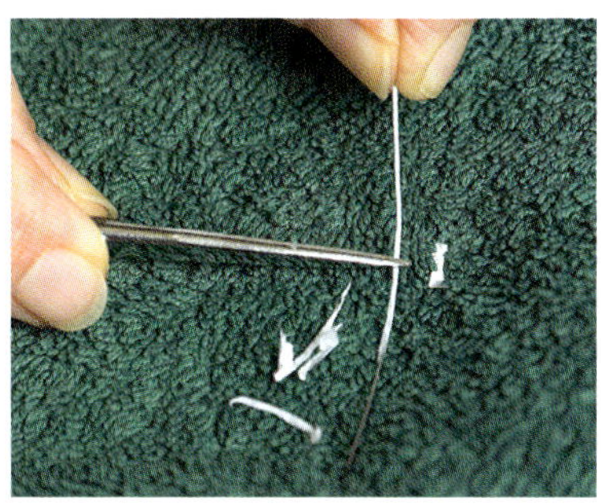

Insert 2 or 3 cm of the wire to the back of the work on the sharp inside tip of the wing. Tape the wire in place with

masking tape, so it is out of the way and won't be caught on your threads as you embroider.

Couch the wire in place every 3-mm or so with the light grey thread. To form a neat edge, angle the needle close to the wire, over, and back into the same hole again. Insert the wire to the back again, cut off the excess wire, leaving a 2 to 3 cm tail and tape in place as before.

Use a buttonhole stitch to cover the wire. Take the needle to the back before inserting it through the loop each time. Angle the needle under the wire for a neat edge.

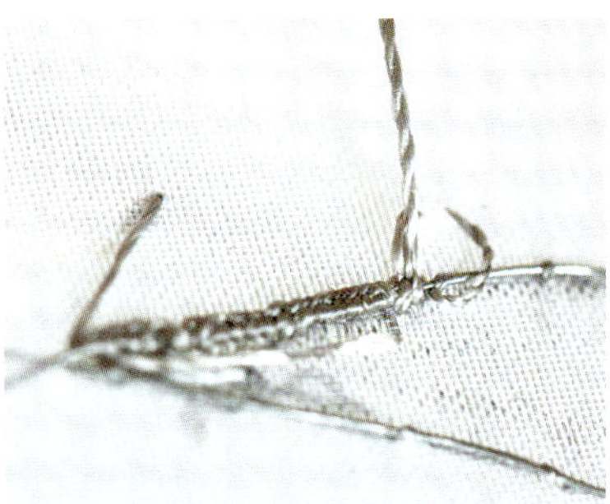

Hint: *When covering wire in buttonhole stitch, start with a knot in the long end of the thread, but ensure the knot is not near the edge of the shape. In this case, use a waste knot. Start a short distance (about 1 cm) outside the shape and make a running stitch to reach the wired edge (the buttonhole stitches will cover and anchor this stitch and the waste knot will be cut away as the wing is cut out.) This way the knot is not visible. To end off, run the thread under or along the inside edge of the wire already covered in buttonhole stitch.*

Form the veins on the wings in the grey thread and short stab stitch. Set the shapes aside to be cut later.

Return to the main design. Thread up with the peacock blue thread and outline the dragonfly's head in tiny stem stitches. Attach two denim blue beads to the head to form the large eyes. Use three anchoring stitches for each bead. Use the same thread and one French knot (two wraps) to form the jaws. Make one more French knot just above the two eyes. Change to the black thread and add a few stab stitches between the knots and beads to outline the eyes and jaws.

Use the same black thread and outline the peacock blue thorax. Form the black curved lines on the thorax in tiny stem or split stitches. Change to the blue thread and use a padded satin stitch to fill in the thorax. First fill in the blue section in tiny stab stitches to pad the shape and then cover with satin stitch, stitching over the black outline for a neat edge. Change back to black thread and form the black outline shapes and curves again in tiny stem or split stitches.

Use the blue thread and a row of small French knots (two wraps) to form the first half of the long, slender, segmented abdomen. Thread up with a denim blue bead and complete the tail by attaching one bead after another in a neat row. Secure each bead with three or four stitches before moving on to the next bead.

Work the six jointed legs in the black thread. The top half of the bent leg is formed with a straight stitch and the bottom half of the bent leg is made in pistil stitch. Stitch into the stem of the flower (Tulbaghia). The one straight leg is completed in pistil stitch.

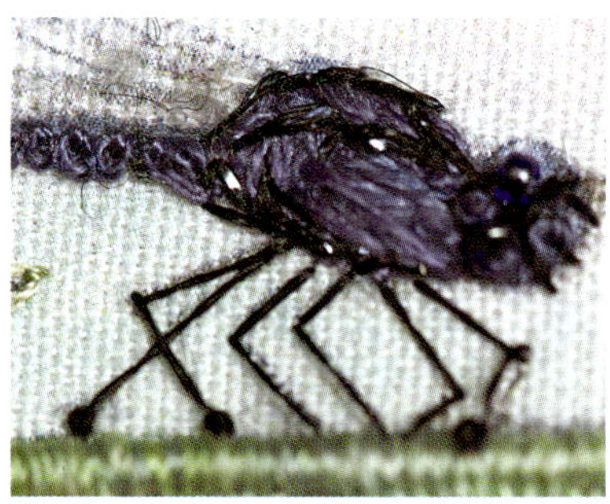

Complete the wings. Remove the tape and cut out the wings. Cut about 5 mm (¼ in) from the edge with small, sharp embroidery scissors, then, once you are holding the wing, cut close to the edge as neatly as possible.

Cut away the waste knot and thread. Dip the wings in a cup of tepid water for thirty seconds or so to dissolve the water-soluble fabric.

The slightly sticky residue left behind works as an anti-fray agent. Allow to dry.

Make a small hole on the main design, just beneath the dragonfly's thorax, with the sharp point of your small embroidery scissors or use a size 16 or 18 Chenille needle. Insert the wires of the bottom wing into this hole until it lies snugly against the fabric. Bend the wires towards the rear so that they are positioned under the wing at the back of the work.

Use the black or blue thread to secure the wire to the back of the work. Secure a length about 0,5 to 1 cm (¼ to ½ in), so the wing does not pull loose. Cut off excess wire with an old pair of scissors or nail clippers. This is to ensure the threads don't catch on the wire ends.

Insert the wires of the top wing into the same hole and attach in place as before, cutting off the excess wires, so they don't catch on your threads as you work the rest of the sampler. Use the grey thread and tiny overcast stitches on the top of the work, at the base of the wings so they are secure and don't flap around too much.

Hint: *Cut a clear cellophane bag to fit the size of each panel. Lay the cellophane on top of the completed panel. Use small running or stab stitches on the line of the blue border to stitch the cellophane to the design. This will protect the delicate wings and embroidery from being damaged or soiled as you work and can be removed once the sampler has been completed.*

PANEL TWO

Penstemon

Wood poppy

Erica

Honeybee

Penstemon digitalis

Common name: beard tongue/beard lip

Penstemon is a large genus of North American and East Asian plants belonging to the figwort family. These herbaceous perennials bear tall spikes of large, brightly-coloured flowers and are excellent for the vase. They are also good plants for landscaping, as many grow in dry conditions and are very frost hardy.

Hint: *This striking flower is ideal for completing a cushion or quilt border, and useful for decorating a trinket box or fire screen. Embroider on a jersey or handbag or embellish a hair band for a special occasion. For scrapbooking and cards, embroider the penstemon on a block of fine wire mesh or cross-stitch fabric, stretch and attach to your page or card with acid-free glue.*

Note: *The penstemon is worked in two parts. The white floral tube is embroidered first with organza ribbon and the foxglove-like petal section is made separately and attached on top of the organza ribbon.*

REQUIREMENTS

20 x 20 cm soft white polycotton or cotton
Brown-tipped stamens

CHAMELEON THREADS

Pure silk: Tropical Green no 3, Spilt Milk no 77, Cyclamen no 22, Scottish Heather no 68, and Rose no 64
Use 1 strand of thread unless otherwise specified

DI VAN NIEKERK'S RIBBONS

Silk ribbon: 4-mm no 82 and 7-mm no 30
Organza ribbon: 15-mm no 104

STITCHES

Straight/stab stitch, straight stitch – twisted, couching, ribbon stitch, blanket/buttonhole stitch, running stitch, buttonhole long and short, long and short stitch, satin stitch, detached chain/lazy daisy stitch, grab stitch

NEEDLES

Use the no 8 crewel needle for 2 strands of thread and the no 9 or no 10 for one strand of thread and beading
Use the no 16 or no 18 chenille for the 15-mm organza ribbon, the no 18 for the 7-mm ribbon, and the no 20 or no 22 for the 4-mm ribbon

Start with the stems. Use the 4-mm green silk ribbon and make a long twisted straight stitch from the base of the stem, over the yellow wood-poppy, inserting the needle into the penstemon.

Bring the needle up a short distance away, on the same flower. Keep the twisted stem quite loose. Couch in place every centimetre or so with green silk thread.

Make another long twisted straight stitch, inserting needle to the back again at the base of the top bud, bring needle to the front again at the top leaf as shown. Couch in place with same green thread.

Hint: *The twisted ribbon tends to make loops at the back of the work. Always check the back once the ribbon has been pulled to the front before making the next stitch and correct if necessary.*

Make the flowers, starting with the floral tubes. Thread up with 16-mm organza ribbon and use a ribbon stitch to make the 4 penstemon tubes.

The closed bud is made with the same stitch with two overlapping each other. Use the grey silk thread to add shadows on top of the organza ribbon stitch of one of the penstemon tubes in straight stitch.

Change to the rose pink thread and work a few pink straight stitches on remaining tubes. Add blanket/buttonhole stitch along the edge of the organza ribbon for an interesting effect.

Change to the darker pink silk and use blanket/buttonhole along the tips of each of the ribbon stitches of the penstemon bud.

Trace the four flower shapes below in the centre of the 20 x 20 cm fabric. Insert in a 15 cm (6 in) hoop. Roll up the four corners and pin or tack out of the way so the corners won't hinder you as you work.

Use the darker pink thread and form a frilly edge on each of the four flowers in long and short buttonhole stitch. Some of the stitches are longer to form the dark pink lines on the shape. Start with a knot at the long end, but ensure the knot is never along the edge of the shape. Always start a short distance inside the white area of the shape and make a few running stitches to reach the outer edge again (the running stitches will be covered with long and short or satin stitch).

Change to two strands of white thread and fill in the centre in long and short or satin stitch. Don't stitch in the darker centre yet; leave this section open, as this will be completed after the stamens have been inserted.

Apply Fray Stop or a tested anti-fray agent and along the pink edges. Cut out a short distance (half a centimetre or so) away from the edge, then once you are able to hold the shape in your hand, cut along the edge as neatly as possible to remove the excess fabric. Take care not to cut into the buttonhole stitches.

Hint: *If this does happen, use the anti-fray agent again to stabilize the stitches. Clear nail polish also does the trick.*

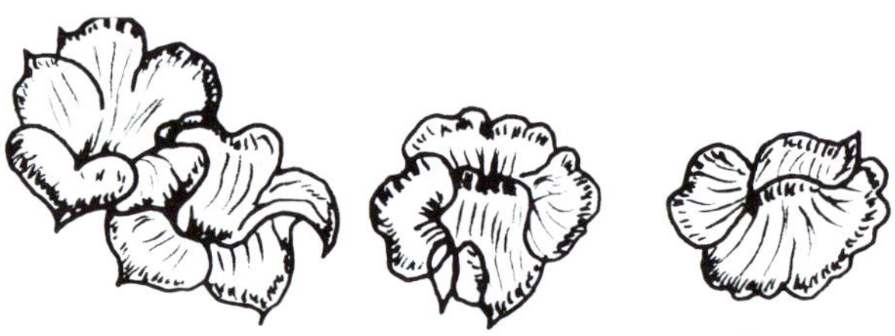

Make two holes a short distance apart in the darker centre of the flower with the sharp point of the small embroidery scissors or the thick no 16 or 18 chenille needle. Cut the stamens in half and insert one in each hole. Alternatively, insert the no 16 chenille needle in the centre of the flower, and thread a folded stamen through the eye of the needle. Gently pull the needle and stamen to the back of the work. Do the same for all four flowers. Bend the stamens at the back and attach with tiny straight/stab stitches in the white thread. Cut off excess stamen lengths. Use the same thread and tiny stab stitches to secure and position the stamens on the right side of each flower.

Use the grey thread and attach each flower shape on top of the organza tube with tiny straight/stab stitches in the very centre, stitching alongside and over the stamens to secure them in place.

Change to the 4-mm green ribbon and form the short stems branching off the main stem in straight/stab stitch. Form the calyx at the base of each flower with the same green ribbon and loose, puffed ribbon stitch.

Hint: *To make a loose, puffed stitch, push the ribbon up as you pierce the ribbon so it makes a higher, puffed, dome shaped stitch.*

Make the smaller teardrop leaves in the 4-mm green ribbon in detached chain/lazy daisy, working over the couched stem as shown. Change to the 7-mm green ribbon and form the larger leaves in the same stitch. Make a grab stitch with the same green ribbon at the base of the large leaf for an interesting effect. Use the green thread and tiny stab stitches to anchor the sides of the stitch to the fabric. This way a large, tidy leaf is formed.

Wood poppy

Stylophorum diphyllum.

A poppy-like perennial, native of Asia and North America. It grows in rich soil in moist woodland conditions and thrives in shade. The attractive yellow flowers with four delicate petals appear in spring and summer on leafy stems. The plant has striking lobed basal leaves. up to 45 cm in length.

Hint: *A cluster of yellow wood-poppies will look so cute on a little girl's dress, or embroidered on a handbag or trinket-box cover. Stitch onto quilt or cushion borders and along the hem of a guest towel. For card-making or scrapbooking, embroider on sheer organza or cross-stitch fabric, stretch, and glue to your page or card with acid-free glue.*

CHAMELEON THREADS

Pure silk: Green Olives no 97, Baked Earth no 7
Goldrush no 37
Use 1 strand of thread unless otherwise specified

DI VAN NIEKERK'S RIBBONS

Silk: 7-mm no 54

STITCHES

Straight/stab stitch, long and short buttonhole, detached chain/lazy daisy, long and short stitch, satin stitch, straight stitch – padded, French knot, stem stitch, back stitch, stem stitch – whipped

NEEDLES

Use the no 9 or no 10 crewel for the threads
Use the no 18 chenille for the 7-mm ribbon

Work the leaves first using the green thread. Start at the tip of the leaf with detached chain and continue down one half of the leaf in long and short buttonhole stitch. Start at the tip again and outline the other half in the same way. Fill in the one half of the leaf with long and short or satin stitch and insert the needle along the central vein each time. Do the same with the remaining half of the leaf.

Hint: *Slant the stitches towards the base of the leaf for a natural finish.*

Work the short stems in straight stitch with the same green thread.

Change to the yellow silk ribbon and form the yellow petals in padded straight stitch. Make a short straight stitch on top of each petal first, and then cover with a longer straight stitch. Keep a loose tension so a rounded petal is formed. Change to the brown thread and use tiny stab stitches to anchor the tips and sides of the yellow petals to the fabric, using the needle and thread to shape the rounded petal.

Change to the gold thread and work tiny French knots (one wrap) to form the golden stamens. Change to the brown thread and add a few brown French knots as before, on the outer edge of the centre. Use the same brown thread and outline the yellow petals along the edge of the fabric, in tiny stem or back stitch to form the shadows.

Erica turgida

Common name: Kenilworth heath/heide

Erica turgida, *a small evergreen shrub with slender branches and small, pointed leaves, grew wild in a small area of the Cape Peninsula in South Africa. Now extinct in the wild, it has been cultivated at Kirstenbosch National Botanical Garden. It bears small, pink cup-shaped flowers with a narrow opening from where the anthers are visible. It flowers in November and December.*

REQUIREMENTS

Mill Hill glass pebble beads no 05145 pale pink

CHAMELEON THREADS

Pure silk: Rustic Brick no 66, Rose no 64 and Charcoal no 15
Use 1 strand of thread unless otherwise specified

DI VAN NIEKERK'S RIBBONS

Silk: 2-mm no 29, 7-mm no 45

STITCHES

Stem stitch, stem stitch – whipped, split stitch, detached chain/lazy daisy, stab stitch, French knot, loop stitch

NEEDLES

Use the no 9 or no 10 crewel for the threads and the no 10 for beading
Use the no 18 and no 20 chenille for the 7-mm ribbon and no 22 or no 24 for the 2-mm ribbon

Use the brown thread and stem or whipped stem stitch for the thicker stems. Instead of making the traditional slanted stitches, use the modern, narrow stem stitch to form a thinner stem, inserting the needle along the drawn line as shown in the stitch gallery on page 159. Long stitches are used (5 to 10 mm or ¼ to ½ in) for a smooth, thin line. Use the same thread and change to split or stem stitch to form the thinner stems.

Thread up with the 2-mm green silk ribbon and form the small leaves growing from the branches in tiny detached chain/lazy daisy stitches. The green leaves on the pink flowers are worked at a later stage.

The cup-shaped flowers are formed over beads to create the raised shapes. Thread up with the pink thread and attach a bead for each pink flower with the opening of the bead facing the branch each time. This is so that once the bead is covered the opening of the flower faces up or downward, not sideward. Attach with five or six-stitches so bead is anchored securely on the fabric.

Thread up with the 7-mm pink ribbon on a no 20 chenille needle. The needle is finer than what is usually used for 7-mm ribbon so that it will fit through the eye of the bead. There is no need for a knot at the long end of the ribbon. Insert the needle in the outer eye of the bead (the part that is farthermost from the branch). Leave a short tail (2 cm/1 in) and cover the bead with three or four stitches as

shown below, overlapping the previous stitch each time. Hold the tail in place with your thumb as you pull the needle through the bead. This way the ribbon wraps tightly around the bead.

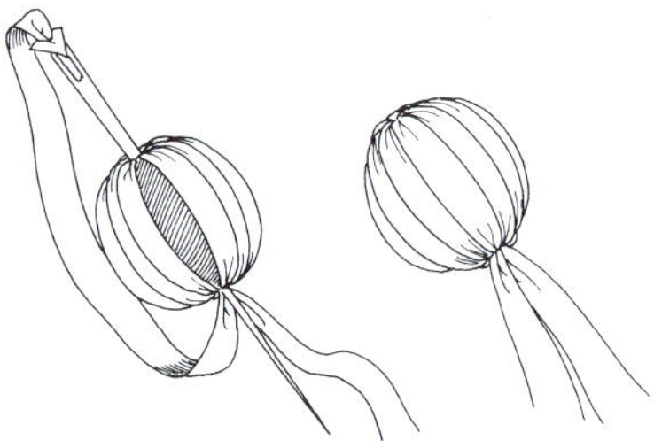

End off by pricking the first tail, so there are two tails on the same side of the bead. Gently pull the tails, so the ribbon remains wrapped around the bead.

Use the pink thread and attach the tails to the background alongside the edge of the bead with tiny stab stitches to form a neat edge. Cut off tails to about 3 mm in length and apply Fray Stop or any good anti-fray agent to the raw edges.

The anthers are made in charcoal thread and two tiny French knots (one wrap) at the base of each pink flower.

Thread a medium-sized embroidery crewel needle with green ribbon (the chenille needle is too thick) and

form the green leaves on top of the pink flowers in loop stitch. Start underneath the bead and stitch through the pink ribbon each time. Use a gentle tension, so the pink ribbon is not pulled out of shape.

Honeybee

Apis mellifera

Honeybee is the common name for a species of insect from the Apiidae family. Honeybees are social insects, forming colonies where they build nests from the wax they secrete. Pollen and nectar are collected from flowers and stored as honey. Honeybees are essential in nature and for agriculture as they pollinate wild plants and crops. Bees are ideal insects for stumpwork as their translucent wings are easy to make and are a charming feature in any project.

Hint: *Use this technique to add that special touch to a beautiful scrapbook page, for card making and on trinket boxes. Embroider on a sheer organza background block. Fold a small seam along the edge of the block (or see page 140 and learn how to burn the edge of the organza block). Use an acid-free glue to attach the organza block to your page or card. Alternatively, use the directions below to embroider this favourite creature onto voile curtains or handbags.*

REQUIREMENTS

20 x 20 cm each white organza and water-soluble fabric
2 Mill Hill beads no 40161, Chrystal White
#30 wire
Fray Stop or anti fray

CHAMELEON THREADS

Pure silk: Scottish Heather no 68, Sunburst no 4, Charcoal no 15
Use 1 strand of thread unless otherwise specified

METALLIC THREADS

Kreinik blending filament no 32 Pearl

STITCHES

Straight/stab stitch, couching, buttonhole stitch, buttonhole open stitch, fly stitch, satin stitch, French knot, pistil stitch, satin stitch

NEEDLES

Use the no 9 crewel for the metallic thread, no 9 or no 10 for the silk threads and no 10 for beading

Use a sharp HB or 2B pencil. Trace the four veined wings below into the centre of the organza block.

Place the organza, pencil side up, on top of the water-soluble fabric block.

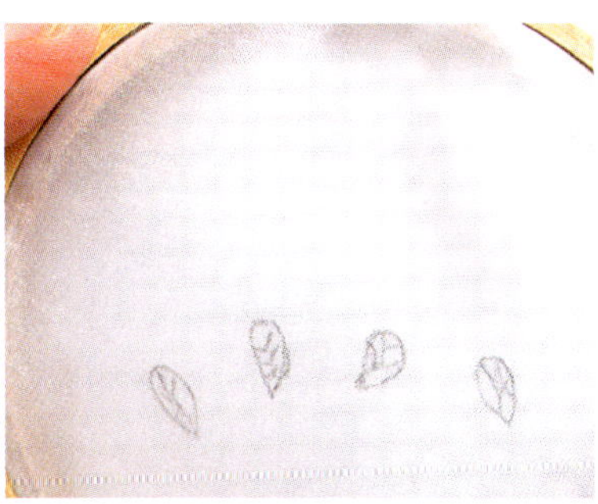

This water-soluble fabric forms a stabilizer for the organza. Insert both layers in the 15 cm (6 in) hoop. Being careful not to tear the water-soluble fabric, gently pull both layers taut and tighten the hoop. Roll or cut the corners away, so they don't hinder you as you work.

See page 21 (Dragonfly) and follow the instructions to strip the coating off the wire. Insert 2 to 3 cm of the wire to the back of the work on the sharp inside tip of the wing. Tape the wire in place with masking tape at the back, so the wire edge is out of the way and won't be caught on your threads as you embroider.

Couch the wire in place every 3 mm or so with the light grey thread. To form a neat edge, angle the needle close to the wire, over, and back into the same hole again. Insert the wire to the back again, cut off the excess wire, leaving a 2 to 3 cm tail and tape in place as before.

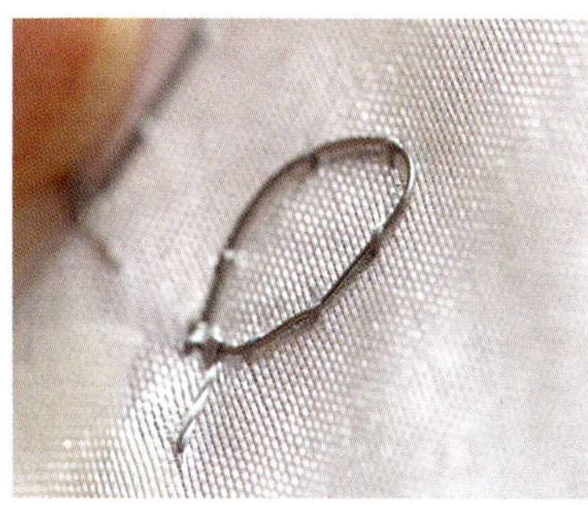

Use buttonhole stitch to cover the wire. Use a longer thread than normal, so the entire wing can be completed with one length of thread. Take the needle to the back before inserting it through the loop each time. Angle the needle under the wire for a neat edge.

Hint: *Start with a knot at the long end, but ensure the knot is not near the edge of the shape. In this case, use a waste knot. Start a short distance (about 1 cm/½ in) outside the shape and make a running stitch to reach the wired edge (the buttonhole stitches will cover and anchor this stitch and the waste knot will be cut away as the wing is cut out). This way the knot is not visible. To end off, run the thread under or along the inside edge of the wire already covered in buttonhole stitch.*

Form the veins on the wings in the pearl metallic thread and open buttonhole stitch or fly stitch. Keep a loose tension for a frilly finish. Remove the tape and cut out the wings. Cut close to the edge with small sharp embroidery scissors. Be careful not to cut the stitches. Dip the wings in a cup of tepid water for thirty seconds or so to dissolve the water-soluble fabric. The slightly sticky residue left behind helps as an anti-fray agent. Set aside to attach later.

Work on the main design. Thread up with the charcoal thread and form the black stripes on the bee's body in tiny satin stitches (vertical-facing head to tail) or French knots (one wrap) made close together. Form the antennae in pistil stitch and the legs in straight stitch. Use the same charcoal thread and a fine no 10 crewel needle and attach a tiny bead to form each eye.

Change to the yellow thread and complete the yellow strips in satin stitch or French knots as before.

Make a small hole on the main design alongside the bee's body with the sharp point of your small embroidery scissors or use a no 16 or 18 Chenille needle. Insert the wires of the two bottom wings into the holes on either side of the body. Bend the wire back on the wrong side of the work, so it lies beneath the wing section and attach in place with small stab stitches. Use nail clippers or old scissors to trim the excess wire, so the threads don't catch as you work.

Do the same for the remaining two wings. Stitch over the buttonhole edge of the wings close to the body to secure them to the design. Use tiny stab stitches in the light grey thread and allow the rounded outer edges to be free, so the wings are lifted off the design. Bend the wings into a pleasing shape.

PANEL THREE

Fynbos

Sunbird

Leucospermum

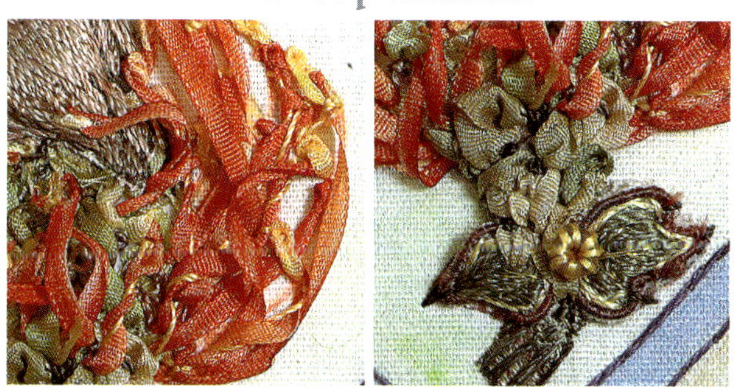

Fynbos

A collective name for thousands of plant species

Plants found in the Cape Floral Region, the smallest and richest of all six floral regions in the world. Typically hard and tough, woody plants with small, leathery leaves, fynbos covers the beautiful valleys and mountains in the South-Western and Southern Cape of South Africa and also includes proteas and ericas, as well as reeds, grasses, bulbs and even pelargoniums. The word fynbos *comes from the Dutch for* fine-leaved.

Hint: *A cluster of these beautiful plants will look good on a handbag or trinket-box cover. Embroider on the borders of a quilt or in the corners of a cushion. Embellish a jersey collar or the hem of a guest towel. Embroider on sheer organza or cross-stitch fabric, stretch, and glue to your scrapbook page or card.*

REQUIREMENTS
Flat, round bead about 4 mm in diameter – rust brown
CHAMELEON THREADS
Pure silk: Rustic Brick no 66, Goldrush no 37 Use 1 strand of thread unless otherwise specified
DI VAN NIEKERK'S RIBBONS
Silk 7-mm no 80
STITCHES
Straight/stab stitch, buttonhole – detached, chain stitch – whipped, ribbon stitch, French knot
NEEDLES
Use the no 8 crewel needle (medium) for 2 strands of thread and no 9 or no 10 (fine) for one strand of thread and beading Use the no 18 chenille for the 7-mm ribbon

Thread up with the brown thread to form the stems of the plants in detached buttonhole or whipped chain stitch. Use tiny stab stitches in a matching thread to catch the embroidered stem to coax the stem into a gentle curve.

Hint: *Many shapes can be enhanced by using a needle and thread to re-shape if necessary. Use a matching thread and tiny stab stitches to 'tell' the shape what to do, for example a leaf that is not attractive or a lazy daisy that is malformed. Simply use stitches afterwards to coax it into shape.*

Change to the green silk ribbon and use ribbon stitch for some leaves and a twisted ribbon stitch for others. (To form a twisted ribbon stitch, see the stitch gallery on page 157).

Change to the golden thread and use a few stab stitches at the tips of each leaf to secure the ribbon and add colour. Small French knots can also be added at the tips for an interesting effect.

Hint: *Keep a loose tension so leaves are loose and puffed.*

Attach a bead at the centre of the leaves to form the cones on the plants. Set the bead on its side and use the gold or green thread to attach the bead. Insert the needle through the eye of the bead, repeating seven or eight times to form a pretty pattern around the bead.

Sunbird

Lesser doublecollared sunbird

From the family Nectariniidae, *sunbirds are small birds found in Africa, the South Pacific and Asia. The species depicted here is* Nectarinia chalybea, *the lesser doublecollared sunbird, native to the fynbos area and evergreen forests in South Africa, where it feeds mainly on nectar of flowers such as the pincushion, and insects. It has a long, thin, curved bill and a tube-shaped tongue. Only the males have the bright, almost metallic colouring shown here, while the females are brownish to yellowish grey. The males build pear-shaped nests, often using spider web for lining and binding.*

Hint: *Make a sunbird to add that special touch to a beautiful scrapbook page or card. Embroider as shown here. Cut out the shape and use an acid-free glue to attach the bird to your paper. Draw the beak on the paper with a black or dark grey fine-liner pen. Stitch the sunbird to quilts, cushions, clothing, and handbags or trinket boxes. You will be pleasantly surprised how easy it is to make this beautiful little bird.*

REQUIREMENTS
20 x 20 cm soft white polycotton or cotton
CHAMELEON THREADS
Pure silk: Forest Green no 32, Cobalt 19, Ruby Red no 65, Rustic Brick no 66, Charcoal no 15. Use 1 strand of thread unless otherwise specified
STITCHES
Straight/stab stitch, stem stitch, split stitch, running stitch, French knot, long and short stitch.
NEEDLES
Use the no 8 Crewel needle for 2 strands of thread and no 9 or 10 for one strand of thread.

Hint: *Pre-printed full-colour panels with the different embroidery shapes can be ordered from our website (www.dicraft.co.za). It is certainly much easier to embroider on a colour-printed image than a line-tracing.*

If you don't have a printed shape, trace the bird in the centre of the white fabric with a sharp HB or 2B pencil. Trace all the direction lines and detail on the bird as neatly as possible to ensure a good finish. Insert the fabric in a 15 cm (6 in) hoop. Pull the fabric taut as a drum and tighten the hoop. Roll up the corners and pin or tack out of the way, so they don't hinder you as you work.

Thread up with Charcoal thread and outline the dark lines on the bird in straight stitch, stem stitch and split stitch. The curved lines are easiest to make in stem stitch or split stitch, and the straight lines in straight stitch.

Hint: *Start with a knot at the long end, but ensure the knot is never along the edge of the shape. Always start a short distance inside the bird shape and make a few running stitches to reach the outer edge again (the running stitches will be covered with long and short stitch) This way the knot is not cut by mistake when the shape is cut out at a later stage.*

Start at the tail and work along the edge. Then embroider the lines on the tail and wings. Add a few straight stitches here and there in the charcoal thread on the blue, red and green sections to create shadows.

Use the Charcoal thread and outline the eye in tiny stem stitches. Add a tiny French knot in the centre of the eye. Wrap thread once around the needle. Use the same thread and straight stitch to form the black line beneath the head.

Change to the green thread and start at the beak. Work down and outwards in long and short stitch, following the direction lines on the shape.

Keep the stitches short, going back to fill in any gaps. Stitch in the same direction as the feathers on the bird for a natural effect. Work into the previous row of stitches each time for a smooth finish.

Change to the blue thread and continue as before, stitching into the green for a smooth finish. Keep following the stitch directions on the shape.

Change to the red thread and fill in the red part of the breast as before.

Fill in the rest of the body in the brown thread working from the red section downwards then change direction slightly and stitch towards the wings.

Use the same brown thread, to fill in the wings and tail feathers in the brown thread starting between the green stitches and working downwards. Keep going back to fill any gaps, stitching in the same direction every time. Don't cover the charcoal lines as these form the shadows that are necessary for a realistic shape.

Apply the anti-fray agent along the edge of the embroidered bird and carefully cut out the shape with small, sharp embroidery scissors. Set the shape aside until the pincushion is ready.

Hint: *Use your fingers to curl the edges down towards the back of the bird. This way the white edges are less conspicuous. Or use a dark brown permanent fabric or laundry marker along the edge to colour in any white fabric that may be showing.*

Leucospermum cordifolium

Common name: pincushion/nodding pincushion/speldekussing

The pincushion is a member of the Proteaceae *family which includes over a hundred species of trees and shrubs found in the Cape region of South Africa. This attractive shrub bears masses of showy, orange flowers for five months from the middle of winter to early summer. Its dome-shaped flower head looks like a pincushion filled with pins. The 'pins' are the long styles that produce pollen at the tips. It is not self-pollinating, but its abundant nectar attracts a variety of insects. Several birds, including the sunbird, then visit the flowers to feed on the insects as well as the nectar. The birds and insects then carry the pollen from one plant to the next. Pincushions are popular garden plants and cut flowers and are available from nurseries all over the world.*

Hint: *This striking flower is ideal for embellishing quilts, handbags, or jerseys. The lovely colours and raised shape of the pincushion will certainly be an interesting focal point in the design. Make the little sunbird on page 35 and add it on top of the pincushion to complete a small, framed picture for someone special, or to embellish a trinket-box cover.*

REQUIREMENTS

Clear tracing paper and HB pencil
Block of white felt and pins
Small strips of toy filling
20 x 20 cm soft white polycotton or cotton
#28 wire
Flat round bead as used for fynbos (see page 34)

CHAMELEON THREADS

Pure silk: Green Olives no 97, Granite no 105, Gold Nugget no 2, Gold rush no 37, Charcoal no 15
Stranded cotton: Baked Earth no 7
Use 1 strand of thread unless otherwise specified

DI VAN NIEKERK'S RIBBONS

Silk 4-mm no 32, and 80, 7-mm no 20
2-mm no 91 and no 53

STITCHES

Straight/stab stitch, stem stitch, split stitch, satin stitch, ribbon stitch, French knot, pistil stitch, couching, running stitch, long and short stitch, long and short buttonhole stitch

NEEDLES

Use the no 8 crewel needle (medium) for 2 strands of thread and no 9 or no 10 for one strand of thread and beading
Use the no 18 chenille for the 7-mm ribbon, the no 20 or no 22 chenille for the 4-mm ribbon, and the no 22 or no 24 for the 2-mm ribbon

Work on the main design and form the thick **stem of the pincushion**. Use two strands of green thread and outline in stem or split stitch.

Fill in the shape with satin stitch, working from side to side, close together, and stitch over the outline stitches. Use the same green thread and make a few straight stitches over the satin stitch in the opposite direction to add more texture.

Use one strand of the black thread and outline the edge on the right in straight stitch to form a shadow.

Form the green **base** and green centre (inflorescence) next. Trace the three shapes above on tracing paper with the HB pencil. Cut out the paper shapes and pin on top of the felt. Cut along the paper edge and remove the tracing paper. Lay the smallest felt shape in the centre of the pincushion. Use the green thread and tiny stab stitches along the edge to secure in place. Place the medium-sized felt shape on top of the first felt layer aligning it so the base of the pincushion is partially covered. Secure in place as before. Lay the largest felt shape on top of the two, aligning the shape with the base of the plant. Secure in place as before.

Now cover the felt shapes. Work alternately with the two green silk ribbons for an interesting texture. Start at the rounded top of the felt shape and use loose, puffed ribbon stitches about 4 mm in length. Work over the edge to cover the felt, continue downwards towards the base.

Change to the 7-mm brown/green ribbon and form larger ribbon stitches at the base. Start at the top and work downwards. Partly cover the previous stitches to build a higher base.

Change to the brown thread and fill the spaces between the ribbon stitches in French knots (two or three wraps) Use the charcoal thread and add a few French knots on the base of the pincushion.

Thread up with the 2-mm orange ribbon and work each style in a loose pistil stitch. Hold the long stem of the pistil stitch with your free hand as you pull the ribbon to the back and front again, to form a loose, curved stitch.

Hint: *Ensure all the tails and knots at the back are secured frequently with thread and tiny stitches. Cut all the excess tails at the back to prevent the pistil stitches from being pulled out of shape.*

Place the little sunbird on top of the pincushion and use the brown thread and tiny stab stitches (about 4 to 5 mm apart) along the edge of the bird to secure it. Work from the tail up, leaving an opening at the head. Fill with tiny strips of felt or small pieces of wadding or toy filling for a natural, three-dimensional look. Close the gap with green thread. Change to charcoal thread and work the beak in rows of stem stitch made close together. If any lines are showing along the bird on the main design, use a matching thread and stem stitch along the edge of the attached bird to extend the shape.

Add more styles (three or four) in the same pistil stitch as before. Use the orange ribbon, this time inserting the needle through the bird, so it appears to be behind the front styles of the pincushion.

Thread up with the darker golden thread and wind around some of the pistils to add more colour. By inserting the needle under and over the pistil stitch each time, and gently tightening the thread around the pistil stitch, some of the styles will appear thinner than others for a realistic finish. Change to the yellow ribbon and add short pistil stitches at the tips of some styles to form the pollen.

Trace the leaves in the centre of the white fabric block, including the stitch direction lines. Use a sharp HB or 2B pencil and draw in all the detail.

Insert in a 15 cm (6 in) hoop. Make a small hole with the no 16 chenille needle at the rounded base of each leaf. Insert 2 cm of the wire in the hole and bend in shape along the drawn pencil line, using tweezers to form a very sharp fold at the tip.

Insert the long wire back in the hole again. Leave a 2 cm tail as before, and cut off the excess wire with a pair of nail clippers or old scissors.

Use a piece of masking tape at the back of the work to cover the raw ends of the wire, ensuring the tape is not covering any area that needs to be stitched.

Use the granite-coloured thread to couch the wire in place every 3 to 4 mm.

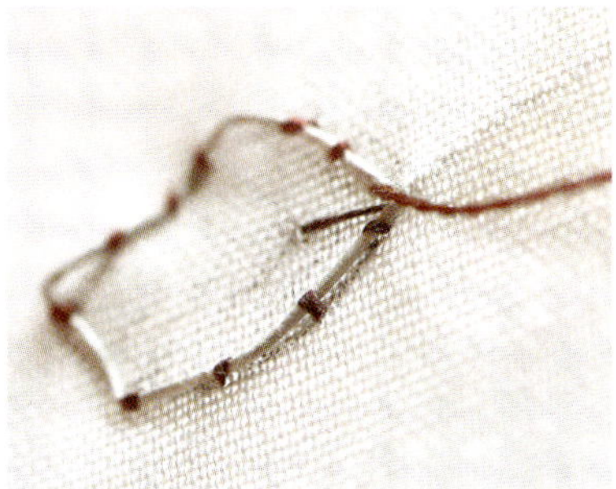

Hint: *Start with a knot and always insert the needle (from the back) inside the shape about 4-mm away from the edge. Make a few small running stitches towards the edge and continue as usual. The running stitches will be covered later with long and short stitch. This way the knot will not be severed when the shape is cut out.*

Use the same thread to cover the wire with buttonhole stitch.

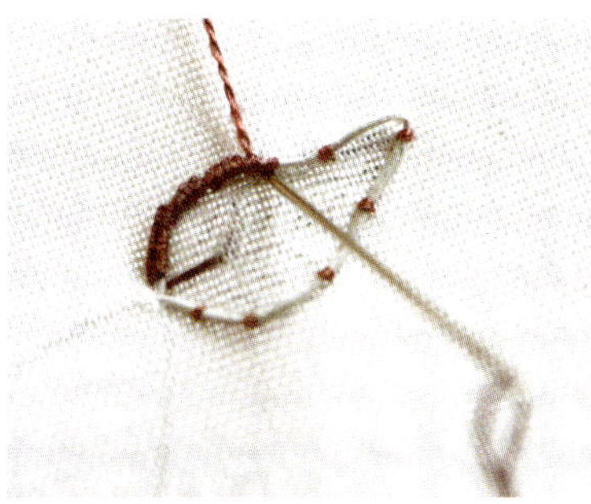

Change to the green thread to fill in the leaf in long and short stitch following the direction lines.

Use the lighter golden thread and stem stitch along the inside edge of the wired leaf.

Use an anti-fray agent and apply along the edge and cut out leaves. Use the no 16 needle or the sharp point of the embroidery scissors to make a hole in the design just beneath the base of the flower. Insert the wires of each leaf into the hole. Bend the wire at the back so each length lies under the back of the leaf and secure with stab stitch. Cut off the excess wire. Use the charcoal thread and stab stitch to form the dark tips of the leaves.

Use one of the green ribbons to add more texture on and above the leaves in ribbon stitch. Finally, attach the flat bead as described for the fynbos plant on page 34.

PANEL FOUR

Wisteria

Camellia

Chameleon

Wisteria sinensis

Common name: Chinese wisteria/bloureën

Native to China, this is the most widely cultivated wisteria, a hardy, vigorous, climbing vine. Cherished for its large sprays of fragrant lavender-blue flowers, the Afrikaans name bloureën, *translated as* blue rain, *is an excellent description of the spring spectacular it offers when flowering. It is a deciduous plant and the flowers appear on bare branches before the leaves. It is a popular pergola plant for the summer shade of is dense foliage. There are also strongly scented white and deep purple varieties, all requiring a sunny position.*

REQUIREMENTS
Mill Hill petite glass beads no 40252
CHAMELEON THREADS
Pure silk: Forest Shade no 33, Black Berry no 8 Use 1 strand of thread unless otherwise specified
DI VAN NIEKERK'S RIBBONS
Silk: 2-mm no 36
STITCHES
Stem stitch – whipped, detached chain/lazy daisy
NEEDLES
Use the no 9 or no 10 (fine) crewel for one strand of thread and no 10 for beading Use the chenille no 22 or no 24 for the 2-mm ribbon

Form the tiny green vines in the green thread and whipped stem stitch. Use the modern, narrow stem stitch (see page 159) rather than the traditional stem stitch to form a finer stem. Keep a tight tension as you whip the stem stitch for a neat finish.

Change to the Black Berry thread and use a no 10 crewel needle to attach the purple beads.

Use three or four anchoring stitches for each bead. Note how the bead only lies upright once the second stitch is made.

Thread up with the green silk ribbon and make a long, thin detached chain/lazy daisy to form each leaf.

Hint: *To form a long, narrow chain, use a tight tension when pulling the loop in shape. Attach with a long anchor stitch.*

Camellia

Camellia japonica

The camellia is a beautiful evergreen ornamental shrub from eastern Asia (Japan, the eastern Himalayas, China and Indochina). It has been in existence for hundreds of years, with a vast number of cultivars produced every year. Colours range from the deepest red, to pink and white, some single, some double, some resembling the rose and the peony. A small group of species from southern China and Vietnam have yellow-bronze flowers. Camellias have between five and nine petals and thick, fleshy, yellow stamens. Camellia japonica *(Japanese camellia) is the best known species. It requires well-drained, acid soil with at least some shade.*

Hint: *Make the camellias for beautiful scrapbook pages, to attach to cards and on trinket boxes. Glue the wooden stems, leaves and petals in place (instead of using stitches) with acid-free multi-purpose glue, adding the flower centres last. To use on jackets or handbags, use the technique described below, working the stems in wool couched in place with a matching thread, but attach the petals to a sheer organza fabric stretched taut in a hoop. Once the leaves, petals and centres have been secured, cut out the flower and fold and stitch excess organza to the back. Add a press stud, so the flower can be removed before washing.*

REQUIREMENTS
Dried twigs (see below) for camellia stems or pieces of brown wool if you would rather not use dried twigs 20 x 20 cm soft white polycotton or cotton 20 x 20 cm medium-weight iron-on interfacing 20 x 20 cm water-soluble fabric Sharp 2B or 3B pencil and water-soluble multipurpose glue stick (similar to the ones used at school)
CHAMELEON THREADS
Pure silk: Forest Green no 32, Egg Yolk no 28, Cyclamen no 22 Stranded cotton: Baked Earth no 7 Gold metallic thread if you would like to add shiny veins on the leaves Use 1 strand of thread unless otherwise specified
DI VAN NIEKERK'S RIBBONS
Silk: 35-mm no 39, 7-mm no 30
STITCHES
Straight/stab stitch, couching, blanket/buttonhole stitch, long and short buttonhole, detached chain/lazy daisy, long and short stitch, satin stitch, chain or stem stitch – whipped, fly stitch, French knot, pistil stitch, back stitch, running stitch, ribbon stitch
NEEDLES
Use the no 8 crewel needle for metallic threads or 2 strands of silk thread and no 9 or no 10 for one strand of thread Use the no 18 chenille needle for the 7-mm ribbon

Form the camellia stems by drying and preserving a few small twigs to add an interesting texture in the design. Tiny wooden stems are quick and easy to attach to the fabric using a matching thread and couching.

The Victorians used twigs, lavender and dried flower cones in their pictures, so using nature's bounty in your embroidery piece is not a new idea.

Use a microwave oven to dry and preserve small branches or twigs. Take a few dried twigs from a shrub in your garden and check that they fit on the design. Branched twigs can be used where there are two or more stems in the design. Place the twigs on two or three layers of paper towel in the microwave oven. Cover with another two layers of paper towel. Microwave on high for 30 to 60 seconds. Take care that the twigs don't burn!

Allow them to dry for a day or two and seal with a clear acrylic spray, floral spray sealer or hair spray.

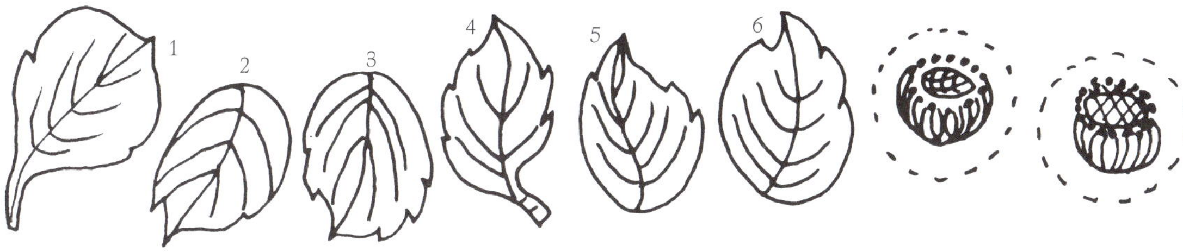

Use the brown thread and couch the twigs (or wool) in place. Place the stem over the chameleon as it will be positioned on top later. Allow the stem to lie a centimetre over the edge of the camellia flowers and buds; these will be applied on top of the twigs in the next step.

If you prefer not to use twigs, form the stem by couching a brown piece of wool in place with a matching thread.

The six leaves and two yellow camellia centres are made separately, then attached to the background.

Trace the six leaves and two centre shapes in the centre of the white fabric. Use a sharp HB or 2B pencil and draw in all the veins on the leaves and stamens on centres – these will be useful direction lines as you embroider. Insert in a 15 cm (6 in) hoop.

There is no need for wire around the edge of these leaves, as they do not need to be bent into shape. Thread up with 2 strands of the green thread and a long and short buttonhole stitch to form a neat edge. Start at the sharp tip with a detached chain and continue down the one half of the leaf in long and short buttonhole stitch. Start at the sharp tip again and outline the other half as before. Fill in the leaf with long and short or satin stitch and insert the needle along the central vein each time. The thick woody stems at the base of some leaves are made at the same time in rows of whipped chain or stem stitch close together.

Hint: *Remember to slant the stitch towards the base of the leaf each time for a natural finish.*

Form the veins on top of the leaves in the brown thread and fly or straight stitch.

Hint: *You may like to use gold metallic thread and the same stitch on some leaves to add interesting highlights.*

Embroider the yellow centres with 2 strands of the yellow thread. Use satin stitch to embroider the rounded oval in the centre in satin stitch. Make another row of satin stitch on top in the opposite direction.

Use the same yellow thread and French knots (one wrap) to form the stamens above and on the side of the centres. Make 2 or more rows in a circular shape. Complete the stamens in the front with pistil stitch and work from the outside upwards. Cut out the centres along the outer broken line and set aside till later.

Apply Fray Stop or anti-fray agent along the edge of the leaves and cut along the buttonhole stitch edge. Be careful not to cut the stitches.

Attach the leaves in position on top of the camellia flowers in the main design, placing each leaf to match the

shape and size of the leaves on the main design. (See numbered diagram on page 46 showing the position of each leaf and petal.) The pink petals of the camellia will be attached on top of the leaves later. Secure the leaves to the design with tiny stab stitches along the rounded base. Stitch along the edges and tips of a few leaves and leave others unstitched along the tips for an interesting variation.

The petals are traced on interfacing which is ironed to pure silk ribbon, cut out and then applied to the design. This is a form of free-standing appliqué. The shapes are easy to make, even for inexperienced needle-crafters, and save a huge amount of the time and effort usually spent on filling shapes with embroidery stitches.

The free-standing appliqué shapes add an interesting texture and combine well with ribbon embroidery and stumpwork.

Trace the shapes below with all the detail on the smooth non-fusible side (not on the shiny or rough side) of the interfacing. Use a soft, sharp 2B or 3B pencil and trace each shape as neatly as possible, leaving a space of about 1 cm (½ in) between the shapes for easy cutting.

Draw in the veins of the petals and number each petal (not the buds) in the same place as on the shapes below (along the rounded base.) This is so the number won't show through the fabric petals on the completed flower. The rounded base is covered by the other petals and flower centre.

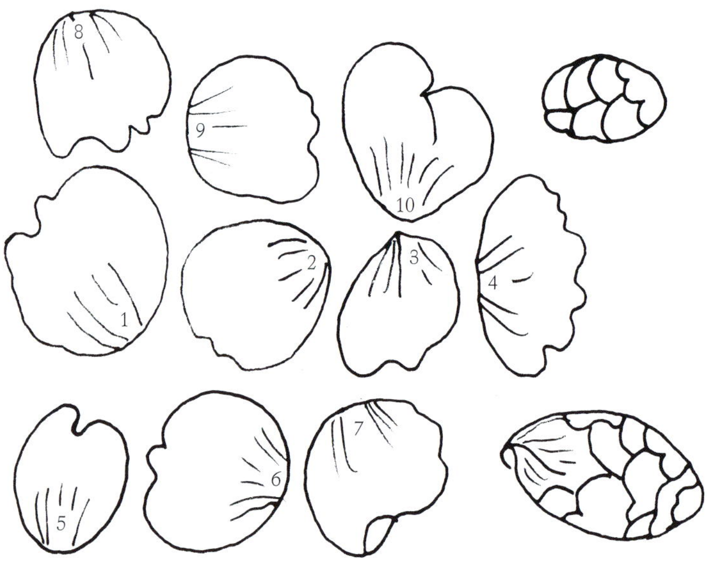

The interfacing shapes will be ironed onto the silk ribbon to prevent the ribbon from fraying and to stabilize the ribbon petals. The petals and buds have been printed in reverse as the shapes are drawn on the wrong side of the interfacing. Once they are ironed to the ribbon and cut out, the petals will be facing the right way.

Cut out the interfacing shapes a few millimetres from the edge. Don't cut on the pencil line yet. To prevent fraying, only cut along the pencil line once the interfacing has been ironed onto the ribbon.

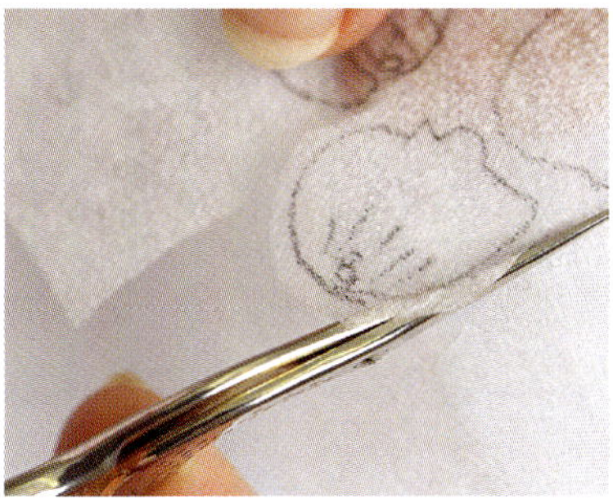

Place the length of ribbon (lightest side up) on the ironing board. Set the iron on a medium setting with the steam off. (A dry iron is essential.) Place a interfacing petal pencil side up (shiny or rough side down) on top of the pink silk ribbon. Press each interfacing petal onto the ribbon so the heat bonds it well. Do the same for all the petals and buds and be careful not to scorch the ribbon. Check that each interfacing shape is attached to the ribbon and that it does not lift at the edges.

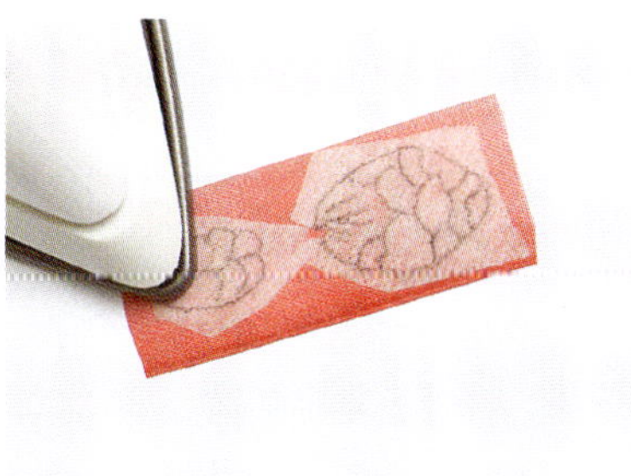

Hint: *If you find your iron has glue residue because you have ironed the wrong side of a petal by mistake, clean it with a tube of hot iron cleaner available from most supermarkets (follow the manufacturer's instructions).*

Cut out each pink shape along the pencil line as neatly as possible with small, sharp embroidery scissors. Hold the petal against a sunny window or light box and only draw in the straight lines (the veins) on the petal. Don't trace the number on the right side. Do the same for the other nine petals. Trace the detail on the two buds too. Keep the shapes in a small bowl, so they don't get lost.

Insert the water-soluble fabric in a 15 cm (6 in) hoop. Place the twelve pink shapes, pencil (interfacing) side down (right side up) on the water-soluble layer. Use a water-soluble multipurpose glue stick (similar to the ones used at school) to lightly glue the shapes to the water-soluble fabric, leaving a 1 cm space between the shapes. Do the same for the two buds. Thread up with the pink thread and work the petals. Use blanket stitch along the edge of every petal. Start at the rounded base with a knot and work anti-clockwise (or clockwise if you are left handed) around each shape. End off with a few back stitches on the base. I only added the blanket stitch as an afterthought once the petals were attached to the main design; this is why your petals will be much neater than mine! Add a few straight stitches on top to form the veins of the petals.

Use the same pink thread and running stitch along the edge of the tip of the large bud. Add a few more stab stitches on the bud (where the green calyx meets the pink)

Change to the green silk ribbon and ribbon stitch. Start with a knot at the back and work from the top down towards the narrow base of the bud. Overlap the stitches for an interesting texture.

End by inserting the needle into the stitches at the back.

Cut out the shapes, leaving a 5 mm (¼ in) edge of water soluble fabric. Place the shapes in a bowl of water for about one minute. Remove and allow the shapes to dry on a towel or dishcloth.

Use the numbered diagram below to place the petals on the main design.

Refer to the number on the back of the petal and position and attach each petal, one by one, in the specified sequence. Use the pink thread and tiny stab stitches at the rounded base to secure the petals in the centre of the camellia. Attach one by one, overlapping the petals as shown in the photographs. The sequence is 2, 3, 5, 4, 1 then 9, 10, 6, 7 and 8.

Attach the buds with the brown thread and tiny stab stitches along the green edge. Add a few straight stitches between the green petals to form the shadows. The pink part of the large bud is not attached to the design. Keeping it loose adds interesting detail.

The yellow centres are prepared as follows: Use the sharp embroidery scissors to cut a few slits in the seam allowance of the embroidered centres. Fold the seams to the back and attach the centre on top of the petals using matching yellow thread and tiny stab stitches.

Chameleon

Bradypodion species (dwarf chameleons)

Unique tree-dwelling lizards found mainly in Africa. Chameleons are famous for their ability to change colour to blend in with their surroundings. The chameleon lives a solitary life, is not endangered but challenged by mankind for habitat and space. Its eyes rotate and can move independently, so it has 360 degree vision. It shoots out its long tongue very rapidly to catch its prey, mainly spiders and insects. Its eggs lay buried in the ground for up to nine months before hatching.

Hint: *Use this technique for something different on a beautiful scrapbook page. Attach this enchanting creature to quilts, clothing, soft furnishings or handbags. See Panel 9 (page 81) for details on making easy stems and branches for the chameleon to hold on to.*

REQUIREMENTS
20 x 20 cm soft white polycotton or cotton
CHAMELEON THREADS
Pure silk: Tropical Green no 3, Gold Nugget no 2, Charcoal no 15 Stranded cotton: Baked Earth no 7 Use 1 strand of thread unless otherwise specified
METALLIC THREADS
Metallic Kreinik blending filament no 32 Pearl
STITCHES
Straight/stab stitch, stem stitch, French knot, back stitch, long and short stitch
NEEDLES
Use the no 9 or no 10 crewel for one strand of silk thread and blending filament

Note: *This chameleon is embroidered separately and then attached to the fabric. You could use the faster appliqué perse-method, printing the shape in full colour and preparing and cutting it out as the frog in Panel 14 (see page 115). The appliqué shape is then cut out and attached as shown on page 48*

Hint: *Pre-printed full-colour panels with the different embroidery shapes are available from our website (www.dicraft.co.za). It is certainly is much easier to embroider on a colour-printed image than a line-tracing.*

If you don't have a printed shape, trace the chameleon shape in the centre of the white fabric with a sharp HB or 2B pencil. Trace all the direction lines and detail on the chameleon as neatly as possible to ensure a good finish. Insert the fabric in a 15 cm (6 in) hoop. Pull the fabric taut as a drum and tighten the hoop.

Roll up the corners and pin or tack out of the way, so they don't hinder you as you work.

Thread up with the brown embroidery thread and form the eye. Outline the eye in tiny back or stem stitch. Add another stab stitch on the corners of the eye. Use pearl metallic thread and form the white section on the eye with tiny French knots, wrapped twice around the needle. Outline the mouth, tail and legs in the brown thread and tiny back stitch. Change to the pale golden thread and start at the mouth. Make three radiating straight stitches to start the long and short stitch.

Fill in the yellow part of the chameleon with long and short stitch, working in the central part of the body. Keep the stitches quite short and irregular in length. (Some stitches are short, others a tiny bit longer to avoid forming a definite ridge or pattern.) Go back into the previous stitches so a smooth texture develops. Every now and then, return and fill in any gaps, but keep stitching in the same direction. Work from head to tail, following the natural shape of the yellow part of the body.

Change to the green thread and fill in the remaining part of the body, following the same process.

Hint: *Always watch the outline of the shape; the outline will tell you when to change direction! As the curved back and tail is stitched, keep the stitches short and change to stem stitch to form curved lines. Keep the stitches very short and bring the needle up at an angle on the widest part of the curve, in other words on the outside of the curve. This way the thread is on the outside and sharp, triangular corners are prevented.*

Fill in the legs and feet, changing direction and using the brown outline on the legs as a guide. Use the same long and short stitch going back into the previous stitches for a smooth finish. Add the brown scales on top of the green and yellow stitches in the brown thread and tiny stab stitches.

Apply Fray Stop or anti-fray agent along the edge of the shape. The tail, legs and feet must be covered with the anti-fray agent too, as these sections are small and fragile. Use the small, sharp embroidery scissors and cut out the shape, leaving a small seam of white fabric. Once the chameleon is cut out and you are holding the shape, neatly cut out the shape, curling the edges backwards so the white edge is not so visible.

Hint: *Use a green fabric marker to colour in the white fabric edge if you prefer.*

Attach the chameleon on top of the stem with a matching green thread and tiny stab stitches along the edge of the toes, chin and tummy. Allow the tail to hang free. Attach with a few stitches on the edge of the back. Fill the shape with bits of toy filling or wadding, using a large tapestry needle or a small, metal nail-file. Take care not to overfill. Close the gap along the top of the head with the same green thread and stab stitch.

PANEL FIVE

L. salignum

L. sessile

Termites

Leucadendron salignum

Common names: Sunshine conebush, geelbos, knoppiesbos

Leucadendron salignum *is the most prevalent species of the* Proteaceae *family in South Africa. Grown for its striking, leathery foliage, it is an eye-catching, dense, evergreen multi-branched shrub about a half to three metres in height. The bracts (leaves) are pointed, some of the older leaves are bright red, some are yellow-tipped with apricot, and others are bright yellow. A variable, drought-tolerant species, it is pollinated by small beetles and grows in well-drained soils from sea-level to 2 000 m or more. This leucadendron flowers in autumn to mid-summer and takes two years to flower from seed. It is a popular cut flower, as the foliage is sometimes red in colour owing to gradual aging of the leaves. Ideal for dried flower arrangements.*

Hint: *Use this technique to add a special touch to a beautiful trinket box and to quilts or wall hangings.*

REQUIREMENTS

20 x 20 cm soft white polycotton or cotton
Sharp HB or 2B pencil

CHAMELEON THREADS

Pure silk: Goldrush no 37, Gold Nugget no 2
Rustic Brick no 66
Stranded cotton: Baked Earth no 7
Use 1 strand of thread unless otherwise specified

NORBILLIE THREADS

Stranded cotton: Salmon no 39

DI VAN NIEKERK'S RIBBONS

Silk: 4-mm no 109, no 23

STITCHES

Couching, detached chain/lazy daisy, straight/stab stitch, stem stitch, ribbon stitch, ribbon stitch – folded and twisted, French knot, running stitch, seeding

NEEDLES

Use no 20 or no 22 chenille needle for the 4-mm silk ribbon, a no 8 or no 9 crewel needle for two strands of thread and no 9 or no 10 crewel for one strand of thread

Start with the stems. The stems are made with dried twigs that are couched in place with brown thread. (See page 42 for instructions on drying and preserving twigs.) Place the twigs on the design, so they overlap a few millimetres into the flower centres – the centres will be added on top later. Couch the twigs in place with 2 strands of the brown or green thread. Couch every centimetre or so to secure.

Use the green silk ribbon and a long, thin detached chain/lazy daisy to form the green leaves. Pull the stitch quite taut before making the anchoring stitch to form a long, thin leaf. Stitch over the twig, so the leaf appears to emerge out of the wood.

Use the same ribbon and a short stab stitch at the base of each leaf for an interesting effect. Thread up with the salmon thread and use a stem stitch along the edge of a few leaves to highlight. Add a few stab stitches at the tips of others for an interesting play with colour.

The yellow bracts (modified leaves that look like the petals of the plant) are made in loose ribbon stitch. Work from the centre outwards and note how some ribbon stitches are twisted, some are folded, others overlap the adjoining stitch. Keep the tension quite loose for an attractive finish.

Use the salmon thread and tiny stab stitches or French knots to anchor the tips of the ribbon stitches to the fabric. This adds the tinge of apricot that makes the plant so attractive and also prevents the ribbon stitches from pulling out of shape.

Trace the three circles below in the centre of the white fabric block.

Trace in all the detail, as these will guide you as you stitch. Remember to trace the outer dotted line around the circles as these will be the gathering lines later. Insert in a 15 cm (6 in) hoop.

Hint: *Go to page 52 to find the line drawing and trace the leaves and centre of the* Leucadendron sessile *at the same time. This will save time later.*

Embroider the three small centres first in the light gold thread and French knots (two wraps) made close together.

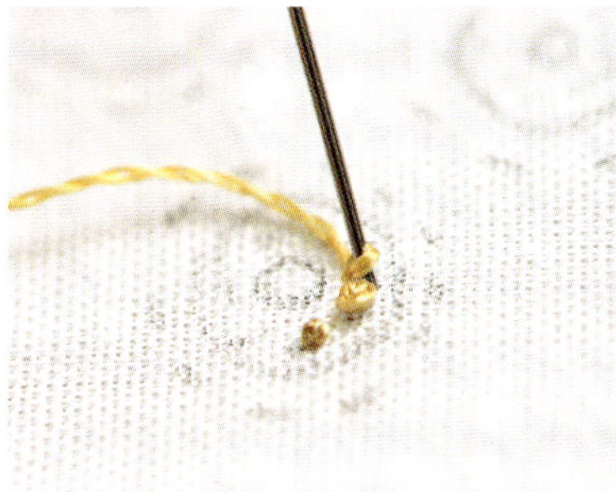

Change to the darker gold thread and add a few French knots between and on top of the light knots.

Change to the brown thread and add a single knot in the centre to form the dark core. End off the thread at the back.

Change to salmon thread and make a knot at the long end. Form a circle of running stitches along the dotted line and don't end off yet. Leave the length of thread hanging and start with a new thread for each circle.

Cut out the circles 2 mm away from the running stitch, but be careful not to cut the thread. Pull the thread to gather the seam to the back.

Use the same thread to anchor the circles on top of each flower. Use tiny stab stitches. Form a circle of French knots around the shape to add colour and shading.

Work the ground. Use the rustic brown thread and tiny stab stitches (seeding) to form the ground behind the termites and flowers.

Leucadendron sessile

Common names: Sun conebush, western sunbush, tolbos

This attractive leucadendron is also a native to South Africa. This plant is an evergreen shrub, not endangered, and reaches heights of 1 to 1,5 m. It is a short, dense shrub with flowerheads that are surrounded by bright yellow bracts (petals) that turn red in July and August in older plants.

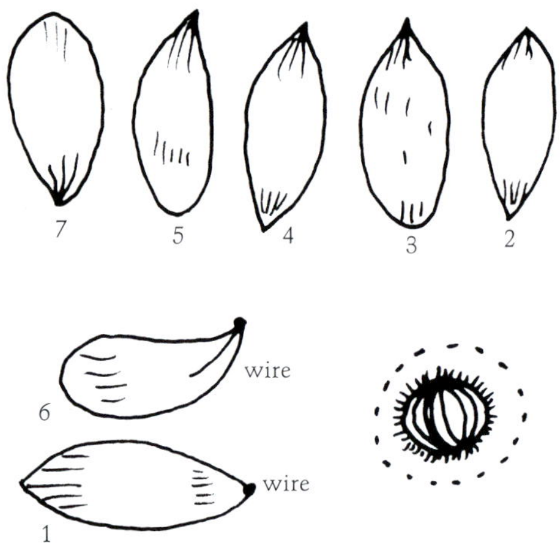

REQUIREMENTS
20 x 20 cm soft white polycotton or cotton Sharp HB or 2B pencil #28 plastic-coated wire (green or white)– from cake decorating stores Fray Stop or anti-fray agent
CHAMELEON THREADS
Pure silk: Goldrush no 37, Gold Nugget no 2, Green Olives no 97 Stranded cotton: Baked Earth no 7, Mango no 50, Golden Green no 36 Use 1 strand of thread unless otherwise specified
NORBILLIE THREADS
Stranded cotton Salmon no 39
STITCHES
Straight/stab stitch, couching, buttonhole- long and short stitch, long and short stitch, bullion knot, French knot, Turkey stitch, running stitch
NEEDLES
Use no 9 or 10 crewel needle for the threads and no 5 (medium) straw/milliner's needle for the bullion knots

Start with the stem, made with a dried twig couched in place with brown thread. (See page 42 for instructions on drying and preserving twigs.) Place the twig on the design, so it overlaps a few millimetres into the flower centre – the centre will be added on top later. Couch the twig in place with two strands of the brown or green thread. Couch every 5 mm (¼ in) or so to secure.

Trace the shapes above in the centre of the white fabric. Use a sharp HB or 2B pencil and draw in all the detail and the numbers on each petal and leaf, including the dotted outer line of the circle. Insert in a 15 cm (6 in) hoop.

Only the yellow bract (petal) number 1 and leaf no 6 have a wired edge as they need to be raised off the design. The remaining petals do not need to be raised and are made separately without a wired edge.

Make a small hole with the no 16 chenille needle at the sharp base of leaf no 6. Use the #28 wire and insert 2 cm of the wire in the hole, bend in shape to cover the edge of the leaf and insert it back in the hole again. Leave a 2 cm tail and cut off the excess wire with a pair of nail clippers or old scissors. Use a piece of masking tape at the back of the work to cover the raw ends of the wire, ensuring the tape is not covering any area that needs to be stitched.

Couch in place every 4 mm or so with the light gold thread.

Hint: *Start with a knot and remember to always insert the needle, inside the shape, about 3 mm away from the edge. Make a small running stitch to the edge and continue as usual. The running stitches will be covered with long and short stitch in the next step. This way the knot will not be severed when the shape is cut out later.*

Cover the wire with long and short buttonhole stitching in the salmon thread along the edge of leaf no 6.

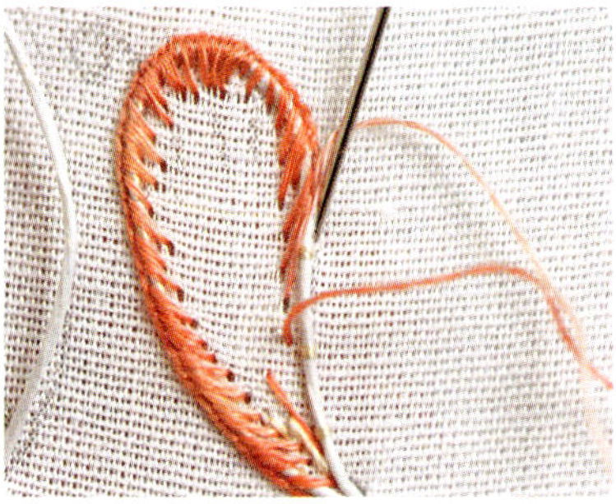

Insert #28 wire at the marked tip of petal 1. Make a small hole with the no 16 chenille needle at the marked tip and insert 2 cm of the wire in the hole, bend in shape to cover the edge of the petal and insert it back in the hole again. Leave a 2-cm tail and cut off the excess wire with a pair of nail clippers or old scissors. Use a piece of masking tape at the back of the work to cover the raw ends of the wire, ensuring the tape is not covering any area that needs to be stitched. Couch in place every 4 mm or so with the light gold thread.

Use the same gold thread for the buttonhole stitch one side and the brown thread on the opposite side.

Continue with long and short stitch and fill in the yellow petal in the mango thread on the rounded curve.

Change to the lighter golden thread and fill in the lighter detail working towards the sharp tip. Use the darker gold thread and add a few straight stitches on top of the light ones, ending in the salmon thread again at the sharp tip.

Change to the darker green olive thread and fill in the leaf shape in long and short stitch working towards the sharp base of the leaf. Change to the golden green thread and add lighter green highlights in the centre continually working to the sharp base.

Fill in the remaining petal shapes as for petal 1, working with a long and short buttonhole stitch along the edge of each shape.

Hint: *Although there is no wire along the edge, the same buttonhole stitch is used for a neat cutting edge.*

Fill in the shapes in long and short stitch, alternating between the salmon and gold threads. Go back to fill in any gaps until a soft, smooth petal is formed. Finally, add brown stab stitches between the buttonhole stitches along the edge and at the tips of some petals for shadows.

Embroider the centre of the flower in bullion knots. Use the straw/milliner's needle and one strand of the dark gold thread and make 7 or 8 bullion knots (use 20 to 25 wraps for each bullion knot) to form the textured centre. Add a few stab stitches in-between the bullion knots in the salmon thread.

Hint: *You may like to remove the fabric from the hoop to make the bullion knots. Some embroiderers like to make bullions on the hoop, to keep both hands free, others prefer to make them off the hoop so that the needle is easier to wrap. See what works for you. If you don't like making bullion knots (many embroiderers don't!), use two strands of the same thread and fill the centre with French knots (2 wraps around the needle).*

Change to two strands of the lighter gold thread and use turkey stitch along the outer edge of the circle (you will need to insert the fabric in the hoop again if you have removed it to form the bullion knots). Make the loops about half a centimetre in length. Trim and fluff every now and then to ensure the texture is not too heavy. End off at the back.

Thread up with the Mango silk thread and make a knot at the long end. Use tiny running stitches along the outer dotted line around the centre. Don't end off. Allow the thread to hang while you cut out the circular shape 2 mm away from the running stitch. Be careful not to cut the thread.

Gather the thread to pull the seam to the back of the shape and anchor the seam with small stab stitches. You will use the same thread to anchor the shape to the flower a little later.

Apply anti-fray agent along the edge of the yellow and green petal shapes and leaf. Begin by cutting out a few millimetres away from the edge to free the shape from the fabric, and then cut out each shape as neatly as possible to remove excess fabric.

As the shape is cut out, refer to the number drawn alongside. Place each shape on top of the numbered petals as indicated below so that it will be easy to identify each shape.

Attach each yellow petal on the design with any matching thread in the following sequence: petal 7 followed by 2, 1, 3, 5, and then 4. Use tiny stab stitches along the base of each shape to anchor it to the design.

Do the same for the green leaf (no 6) attaching it to the wooden twig. The needle will glide quite easily through the wood, but ensure it is a fine no 9 or 10 needle. If the twig splits, use a tight couching stitch over the twig to anchor the split edges together.

Place the centre of the flower on top of the petals and use the Mango thread and tiny stab stitches to secure it in place. Add the orange shadows on the edge of the centre in the same Mango thread and French knots (two wraps).

Termites

Insect order: Isoptera

The name Isoptera *(*iso- *meaning* equal*;* -ptera *meaning* wing*) was given to insects that possess two pairs of wings that are equal in length. Termites, also known as white ants, are among the most important insects on earth, as they play a vital role in breaking down dead plant material. They are social insects and build large communal nests that house an entire colony. They have hair-like antennae (about as long as the head) and thick waists which distinguish them from ants. Termites are most closely related to the cockroaches.*

Hint: *Embroider the termites on quilts, cushions, clothing, or handbags to add a special touch or glue to a beautiful scrapbook page, card or tissue-box covers using acid-free glue and draw the legs and antennae with a black fine liner.*

REQUIREMENTS

20 x 20 cm soft white polycotton or cotton
Sharp HB or 2B pencil
Fray Stop or any clear-drying anti-fray agent

CHAMELEON THREADS

Pure silk: Charcoal no 15, Flame Lily no 31, Goldrush no 37, Gold Nugget no 2.
Use 1 strand of thread unless otherwise specified

STITCHES

Straight/stab stitches, seeding, stem or split stitch, satin stitch, bullion knot, pistil stitch.

NEEDLES

Use a no 5 (medium) milliner's/straw needle for the bullion knots and no 9 or no 10 crewel needle for the rest

Start with the bodies. Trace the shapes above on the white fabric, using a sharp HB or 2B pencil. Trace all the detail as neatly as possible. Place the fabric in a 15 cm (6 in) hoop and roll up the corners, so they don't get in the way as you work. Pin or tack them in place. Thread up with the flame thread and outline the head in tiny stem or split stitch

Fill the head with tiny seeding stitches. Cover the seeding stitches in satin stitch, working from the neck towards the mouth. Stitch over the outline stitch so the satin stitch is padded and a raised shape is formed.

The body is worked in bullion knots. Use the medium milliner's/straw needle and form the bullions in the darker gold thread.

Change to the light gold thread and fill in the remaining area in satin stitch adding brown stab stitches between the bullions for shadows.

Apply anti-fray agent along the edge and cut out as you did for the leucadendron petals (see page 54). Attach the shapes to the background, using the light gold thread and tiny stab stitches. The head is anchored in the same way, but use the Flame thread.

Thread up with the black thread and form an outline along the body and head in stem or split stitch. Form the legs in stab stitch for the short top section and pistil stitch for the long straight lines. The antennae are made in pistil stitch. Work from the orange part of the head outwards.

PANEL SIX

Restio

Felicia

Strelitzia

Butterfly

Restio

Restio multiflorus

This grass-like plant belongs to the reed family. Multiflorus *means* with many flowers *and refers to the mass of light green stems which are covered in dense, gold and dark brown bracts for most of the year and looks like a mass of flowers. The actual flowers, borne for a short period, differ on the male and female plants and are pure white on the female and yellow green on the male plants. The plant grows wild in South Africa to a height of 1 to 1,5 m and is pollinated by wind.* Restio multiflorus *likes the wet winters and long dry summers of the South-Western Cape. It has become quite popular as a garden and landscaping plant*

Hint: *Embroider this indigenous grass on jerseys, cushions, linen, guest towels and clothing to add that special rustic touch.*

REQUIREMENTS
Mill Hill petite glass beads no 42030
CHAMELEON THREADS
Pure silk: Pine Needles no 61, Rustic Brick no 66 Use 1 strand of thread unless otherwise specified
DI VAN NIEKERK'S RIBBONS
Silk 4-mm no 110
STITCHES
Straight/stab stitch, chain stitch – whipped, French knot, detached chain/lazy daisy, stem or split stitch, grab stitch
NEEDLES
Use the no 9 or no 10 (fine) crewel needle for one strand of thread and the no 10 for the beads Use the no 20 or no 22 chenille needle for the 4-mm ribbon

Start with the stems. Thread up with the green thread and use a whipped chain stitch. Start at the base and work up to the tip, stitching over the bracts and flowers as these will be added on top later.

Thread up with the brown thread on the finest no 10 needle and attach a bead on top of each flower with three or four anchoring stitches. Add a few small brown French knots (one wrap) in-between the beads. Change to the green thread and add a few more green French knots between the beads.

Thread up with the cream silk ribbon and use a detached chain/lazy daisy to form the bracts. Work from the stem outwards. Change to the brown thread and work tiny stab stitches at the tip of each bract for a natural finish. Use the same brown thread and fine stem or split stitch alongside the leaves to form the shadows. Add the brown knots at the base where the bract emerges from the stem in grab stitch or stab stitch

Felicia amelloides

Common names: Paris daisy, blue marguerite, bloumagriet

A hardy, fast-growing, evergreen perennial bearing beautiful blue, daisy-like flowers with striking bright yellow centres for prolonged periods from late summer to autumn. It occurs naturally in South Africa, but is cultivated all over the world. Usually frost and wind resistant, it needs full sun and does not require a lot of water. It tends to become scraggly and needs regular pruning and dead-heading to extend the flowering period. Wonderful plants for the garden and for containers on the patio as they do not close up at night (as many flowering plants do).

Hint: *Use the 2-mm silk ribbon and no 24 chenille needle to stitch these easy to make daisies on a page of hand made paper. Use this unique page for card-making or for an attractive scrapbook page. Keep a gentle tension throughout and complete by stitching or gluing a yellow bead in the centre with acid-free glue. Embroider on jerseys, cushions, linen and clothing to add a special touch.*

CHAMELEON THREADS
Pure silk: Green Olives no 97, Goldrush no 37 Use 1 strand of thread unless otherwise specified
DI VAN NIEKERK'S RIBBONS
Silk 2-mm no 81
STITCHES
Buttonhole-detached or stem stitch – whipped, detached chain/lazy daisy, French knot
NEEDLES
Use the no 9 or no 10 (fine) crewel needle for one strand of thread Use the no 22 or 24 chenille needle for the 2-mm ribbon

Work the stems first. Use the green thread and detached buttonhole or whipped stem stitch, to form the thin, curved stems.

Change to the 2-mm ribbon and work each petal in long, thin detached chain/lazy daisy stitch. Pull the ribbon quite taut to form a thin elongated chain.

Add the yellow centre on each daisy. Use the golden thread and a French knot (two or three wraps).

Strelitzia reginae

Common name: Crane flower/bird of paradise/kraanvoëlblom

A slow-growing, evergreen perennial, famous for its impressive flowers which stay on the plant for many months. Indigenous to South Africa where it occurs naturally in the Eastern Cape, and one of the country's best export products to the extent that it is the emblem flower of the city of Los Angeles! Tropical in appearance with long, thin, pointed upright leaves, it has bright orange sepals and blue petals in a green, boat-shaped spathe or bract edged with red. It is well-loved by sunbirds. When a bird sits on the flowers to sip the nectar, the blue petals open and cover the bird's feet in pollen. The strelitzia has no perfume but makes a striking cut flower that will last several weeks in a vase. It is frost tender and sensitive to cold.

Hint: *This striking flower is worked using the barbola technique, and is ideal for embellishing wall quilts, handbags, trinket boxes or jerseys. Its detached orange and blue sepals will certainly be an interesting focal point on any project.*

REQUIREMENTS
2 x 20 x 20 cm soft white polycotton or cotton Sharp HB or 2B pencil Fray Stop or anti-fray agent
CHAMELEON THREADS
Pure silk: Green Apples no 40, Rose no 64, Emerald no 101, Nasturtiums no 56, Flame Lily no 31, Peacock no 103, Knysna Forest no 3 Stranded cotton: Mango no 50, Moss no 54, Pinotage no 100, Baked Earth no 7 Use 1 strand of thread unless otherwise specified
NORBILLIE THREADS
Stranded cotton: Salmon no 39
RAJMAHAL ART SILK
Lagerfeld Ink no 25 or no 29 Charcoal
STITCHES
Straight/stab stitches, stem stitch, stem stitch filling, French knot, detached chain/lazy daisy and overcast stitch
NEEDLES
Use no 9 or no 10 crewel needle for one strand and no 8 or no 9 for two strands of thread

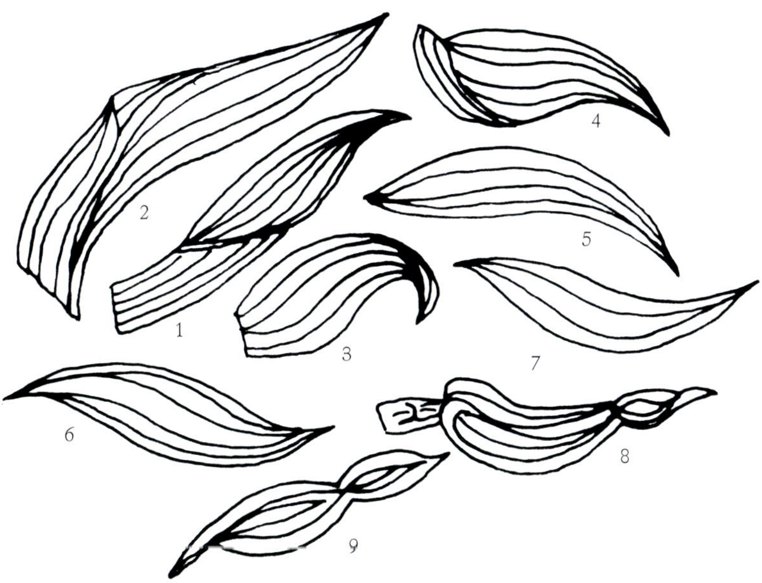

Trace the petals, sepals, spathes and leaves in the centre of one of the white fabric blocks as neatly as possible with the HB or 2B pencil. Number on the outside of each shape (from 1 to 9) and carefully trace the direction lines inside each shape for easy reference later.

Hint: *At the same time, trace the wings of the butterfly to save time. Set aside and work as described on page 63.*

Centre the block with the traced petals on top of the second fabric block and insert both layers in a 15 cm (6 in) hoop. Pull the layers taut as a drum and tighten the hoop. Roll up the corners and pin or tack out of the way, so they don't hinder you as you work. The Barbola technique is used to make the petals.

Start with shape 1. Use 2 strands of no 40 green silk thread and work through both layers of fabric. Outline the edge of the shape in stem stitch. Fill in the shape with row after row of stem stitch filling made close together (see stem stitch filling page 159). Go back and fill in the gaps with straight/stab stitch.

Hint: *Remember to start the knots inside the shape so they won't be cut when the shape is cut out later (see sunbird, page 35 for more details).*

Use two strands no 54 stranded cotton and add short rows of stem stitch between the previous rows of stem stitch along the edge and in the centre of the shape to add darker shadows.

Barbola is an ancient Tibetan form of stumpwork, where layers of fabric are used to create embroidered shapes. Layers of pre-cut fabric shapes are pasted one on top of one another to create an embossed, three-dimensional sculpture. In this panel, the strelitzia petals and sepals are made on two layers of fabric then cut out and used as a sculpture form. No wiring is used; instead, a fabric stiffener such as an anti-fray agent or glue paste is used to stiffen and strengthen the shapes before they are attached to the main embroidery. The shapes are made a tiny bit bigger than normal, so the cut out shapes can be moulded to form a convex, concave or curved shape. This way the shape is elevated on the design – a form of raised embroidery or stumpwork. It is a surprisingly easy form of stumpwork and saves a great of deal time, as no wire needs to be attached and covered.

Change to one strand of the pink silk thread and embroider the curved pink line in stem stitch. Make two or three rows close together.

Hint: *Keep the stitches quite short (about 4 to 6 mm in length) as longer stitches can be untidy once the shape is cut out and attached to the fabric.*

Embroider shape 2. Use the same pink thread and a row of stem stitch along the centre of the shape.

Change to two strands of the stranded cotton no 100 and fill in the wine red sections as before. If the pink line has been covered with the Wine Red stitches, make another row of stem stitch down the centre of the shape. Change to the emerald green silk thread and add the rich green section on the right in stem stitch, forming closely packed rows of stem stitch as before.

Embroider shapes 8 and 9 (the blue petals). Thread up with 1 strand of Pacock Blue silk and work the blue shapes, outlining in stem stitch and filling in with closely packed rows of stem stitch.

Thread up with the black thread and embroider the curved black base of shape 8 in tiny stem stitches. Add a few black straight stitches beneath this curve to form the dark shadows on the narrow peduncle of this petal. Change to the pink thread and form one or two French knots inbetween the black shadows on the peduncle. Add the pink vein higher up in detached chain/lazy daisy stitch. Use the same pink thread and stem stitch to add a centre vein on shape 9.

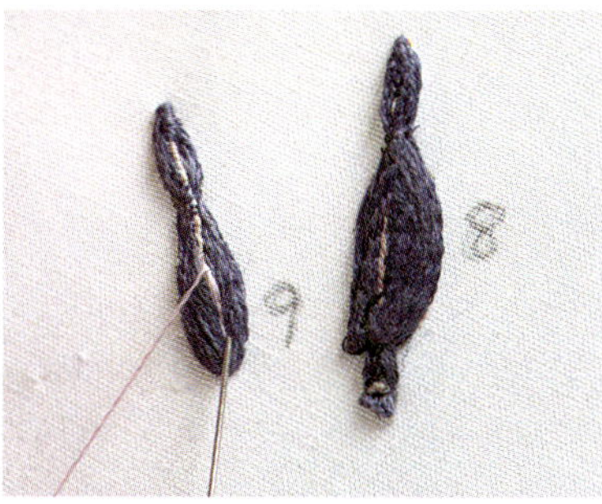

Now work the orange sepals. Thread up with two strands of the flame lily silk thread and outline each of the five shapes in stem stitch. Change to the moss green thread and add two or three rows of green on the right edge of sepals 7 and 6 and the tip of sepal 5. Fill in the sepals with rows of stem stitch made close together, alternating between the nasturtium, salmon and mango threads. Go back and fill any gaps with straight stitch.

Thread up again with one strand of the flame lily thread and add the darker veins in stem and straight stitch. Finally use the black thread and work straight stitch at the base and stem stitch along the edge of petal 4 to add the black shadows.

Apply an anti-fray agent that dries clear (test first!) along the edges as well as to the embroidered sections of all the shapes. The entire shape needs to be covered with the liquid. First cut out each shape a distance away from the edge, then neaten by trimming the fabric as close to the stitches as possible.

Once all nine shapes have been neatly cut out, use a black laundry marker along the white edge of shapes 1, 2, 4, 7, 8 and 9 to form a dark shadow.

First attach shape 2. Thread up with the Pinotage thread and make a knot at the long end. Bring the thread up along the wine-coloured edge on the main design. Wet the shape again with the anti-fray agent and while still damp, pinch the shape between your thumb and forefinger, bending it downward, so a rounded dome shape is formed. Attach the shape to the fabric with tiny stab stitches about 4 mm apart.

Keep pinching the spathe with your free hand so it keeps its curved shape. Use the same thread to anchor the spathe along the green edge with the same stitch, aligning the shape with the edge on the design.

At the sharp tip, use the moss green thread and a few straight stitches to anchor the tip to the background.

Hint: *If you are making the butterfly in this panel, complete the wings first before cutting out any shapes. See page 63 for step by step instructions.*

Wet shape 1 and form a curved spathe as before. Refer to the numbered diagram above and line up shape 1 on the design, overlapping shape 2 slightly. Use the moss green thread to anchor along the sides as before.

Attach the blue petal on the right (shape 9). Thread up with the blue thread and attach at the base of the shape in the centre of the strelitzia on the design. Use a few stab stitches along the edge, but leave the tip unattached. Thread up with the pink thread and use an overcast stitch along the narrowed section to complete this step.

Thread up with the no 3 green silk and insert the needle from the back in the centre of the strelitzia. Wet the orange sepals a bit, so they are easier to bend into shape. Place sepal 4 on the design. The sepal is attached at the base and only one side (any side) with a few straight or stab stitch in the green thread.

Use the following sequence and attach the other sepals in the same way, 5, 6, 7 (overlapping no 9) and lastly attach no 3. Add a few more stab stitches in the green thread to form the shadows in the centre. Finally, add the blue no 8 petal on top.

Use the black thread and attach the shape in the centre and along the narrowed section at the tip of the shape.

Butterfly

Butterfly order: Lepidoptera

There are about 150 000 butterfly and moth species worldwide, both from the order Lepidoptera. *Butterflies are flying insects with large, beautiful, colourful wings that magnetize children and adults alike. The wings are colourful owing to the loose powdery scales that rub off when touched. Like all insects, butterflies have six legs. Their long, thin body is divided into a head, a thorax and an abdomen and they have two knobbed antennae. Butterflies are a significant part of conservation as they pollinate plants. They fly during the day and rest at night with their wings held erect. Many butterflies migrate to avoid cold winters.*

Hint: *This beautiful creature is ideal for an eye-catching scrapbook page, card or to attach to voile curtains. Use to embellish wall quilts, handbags, trinket boxes or jerseys. Follow the steps below and learn how easy it is to create this much-loved insect.*

REQUIREMENTS
20 x 20 cm soft white polycotton or cotton Sharp HB or 2B pencil #30 wire-white or green from cake decorating shop Brown or black-tipped stamen from cake decorating shop Fray Stop or anti-fray agent
CHAMELEON THREADS
Pure silk: Egg Yolk no 28, Cobalt no 19, Rustic Brick no 66. Use 1 strand of thread unless otherwise specified
RAJMAHAL ART SILK
No 25 Lagerfeld Ink or no 29 Charcoal
STITCHES
Straight/stab stitch, couching, buttonhole stitch, buttonhole-long and short stitch, satin stitch, French knot
NEEDLES
Use no 9 or 10 crewel needle for one strand of thread

Hint: *Pre-printed full-colour panels with the different embroidery shapes are available in from our website (www.di-craft.co.za). It is certainly is much easier to embroider on a colour-printed image than a line-tracing.*

If you don't have a printed shape, trace the two wings in the centre of the white fabric with a sharp HB or 2B pencil. Trace all the direction lines and detail on the butterfly as neatly as possible to ensure a good finish. Insert the fabric in a 15 cm (6 in) hoop. Pull the fabric taut as a drum and tighten the hoop. Roll up the corners and pin or tack out of the way so they don't hinder you as you work.

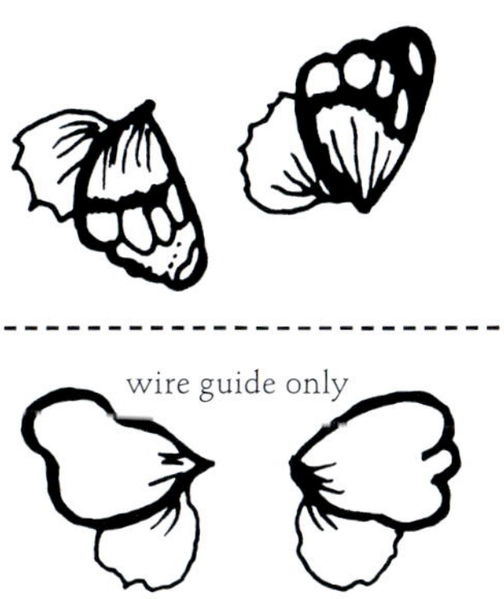

Use the #30 wire for the wings. Refer to the diagram on the left and note that only the fore wings are edged with wire (the thick black line on the diagram.) The hind wings are not wired and buttonhole stitch is used to form a neat edge. Insert 2 to 3 cm of the wire to the back of the work on the sharp point of the wing. Tape the wire in place with masking tape, so it is out of the way and won't be caught on your threads as you embroider.

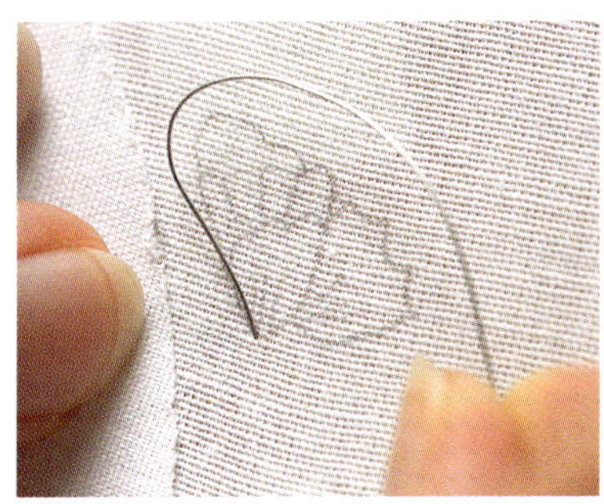

Hint: *First strip the plastic coating off the wire by holding the wire on a towel or dishcloth. Use the outer blunt edge of an old pair of scissors and run the scissors over the wire to strip the coating. This way the wire is finer and not too thick for the delicate wings.*

Couch the wire in place every 3 mm or so with the black thread. To form a neat edge, angle the needle close to the wire, over, and back into the same hole again. Insert the wire to the back again and tape in place as before. Use a buttonhole stitch to cover the wire (see buttonhole stitch over wire page 153). Take the needle to the back before inserting it through the loop each time. Angle the needle under the wire for a neat edge.

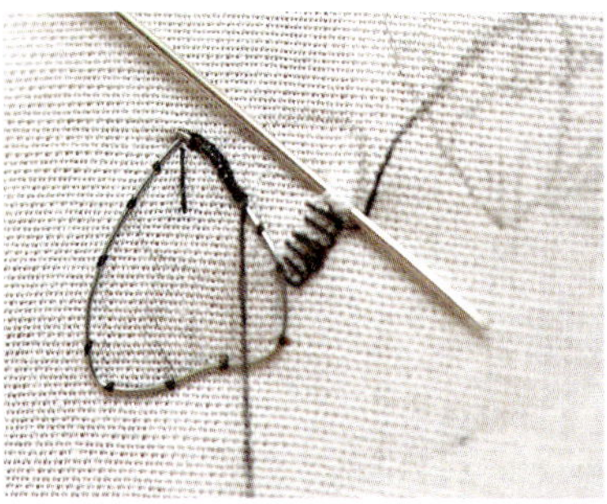

Hint: *Start with a knot at the long end, but ensure the knot is never along the edge of the shape. Always start a short distance inside the wing and make a running stitch to reach the outer edge again (the running stitch will be covered with stitches later). This way the knot is not cut by mistake when the shape is cut out at a later stage.*

Use a long and short buttonhole stitch to form the edge of the hindwings and the same black thread to fill in the black outline of the scales in tiny straight/stab stitches. Change to the yellow thread and fill in the yellow sections in satin stitch. Finally use the blue thread and fill in the blue parts. Thread up with the blue metallic thread and add a few straight stitches on top of the embroidered blue section for highlights.

Work on the main design. Thread up with the brown thread and form the brown body in French knots (1 wrap) made close together. Add a few knots on the outside edge in the black thread making one knot beneath the other to form the sharp tip of the abdomen. Make two French knots on the head to form the eyes.

Cut out the wings. Remove the tape and apply an anti-fray agent along the edge. Cut close to the edge with small, sharp embroidery scissors. Be careful not to cut the stitches. Use a black laundry marker and draw along the edge to cover the white fabric.

Make a small hole on the main design alongside the butterfly's body with the sharp point of your small embroidery scissors or use a size 16 or 18 chenille needle. Place the two wings on either side of the body, one at a time, by inserting the wire ends into the holes just formed. Bend the wire backwards at the back of the work so it lies beneath the wing section, and attach in place with small stab stitches. Use the nail clippers or old scissors to trim the wire edges. This is so that the threads don't catch on the wire ends. Secure the hindwings along the buttonhole edge with tiny stab stitches in the black thread to attach them to the design and allow the forewings to be free. Bend the wings into a pleasing shape.

Attach the stamen to form the antennae. Use a no 18 chenille needle (or the sharp tip of the small embroidery scissors) to make a small hole in the design. Fold the stamen in half and insert the folded stamen in the hole. Alternatively, fold the stamen in half and thread the folded section through the eye of the needle. Take the needle to the back, working with a gentle tension. Hold on to the stamen tips on the right side, so they are not pulled through by mistake. Gently pull the stamen back to the front until you are happy with the length. Use the black thread and tiny overcast stitches at the base of the antennae to secure in place. Bend the folded white part of the stamen at the back of the work and anchor in place with stab stitches. Cut off the excess string, ensuring that there are no raw ends to catch on your threads later.

PANEL SEVEN

Phlox

Pimpernel

Rose

Butterfly

Phlox divaricata

Common name: Wild sweet William, blue phlox, floksies

An evergreen perennial native to Eastern North America. Grows in moist, fertile shaded areas on the outside edge of forests in sun to light shade. A fragrant groundcover about 25 to 50 cm high that attracts moths at night and hummingbirds, butterflies, and bees in the daytime. Phlox need a constant supply of nutrients and this is why they thrive in woodlands. Clusters of tubular flowers appear in spring and early summer. The flowers have five petals shaped like a slice or wedge of cake and vary in colour from light blue, to periwinkle and lavender. Stems are slender, hairy and sticky and grow outward to form a loose mat. The oval leaves are 2,5 to 5 cm long and favoured by red spider-mite.

Hint: *Embroider this interesting flower to add a special touch to a beautiful scrapbook page, or for a card. Embroider on a cotton or organza background, stretch and mount before gluing to the page or card. Embroider directly on a handbag or jersey or a cloth cover for a trinket box.*

REQUIREMENTS
Mill Hill Glass seed beads: 02053 (green)
CHAMELEON THREADS
Pure silk: Knysna Forest no 3, Black Berry no 8 Use 1 strand of thread unless otherwise specified
DI VAN NIEKERK'S RIBBONS
Silk: 7-mm no 63, 2-mm no 15, no 29 or a small piece of soft green wool for the stems
STITCHES
Couching, back stitch, loop stitch, ribbon stitch, straight stitch – padded, detached chain/lazy daisy, stab stitch, and fly stitch.
NEEDLES
Use the no 9 or no 10 crewel for one strand of thread and no 10 for the beads; use the no 18 or no 20 chenille for the 7-mm ribbon and 22 or 24 for the wool and 2-mm ribbon

Start with the stems. Thread up with the wool or no 29 silk ribbon and insert the needle one centimetre beneath the rose, at the base of the stem. Work over the rose and the blue flowers, as they will be completed over the stem later.

Couch the wool or ribbon in place with the green thread. Work to the end of the top flower. Use the same wool and back stitch to form the stems branching off the main stem.

Form the blue petals next. Thread up with the blue ribbon and start in the centre of the flower. Make a loop stitch for each petal. Form the loop over a large tapestry needle (or similar object) and hold the loop in place with the needle until the next stitch is made. Move the needle to make the next stitch. Work with a gentle tension so the previous stitch is not pulled out of shape.

Hint: *Ribbon stitch and padded straight stitch are both good substitutes for loop stitch.*

Form the two closed buds in the same ribbon and detached chain/lazy daisy.

Change to the Black Berry thread and use tiny stab stitches at the tips and sides of the petals to anchor and shape the petals. Use the same thread and repeat the stab stitches at the base of each petal (in the centre of the flower) to secure the petals and to add the dark purple veins.

Add one green bead in the centre of three blue flowers. Note that the top flower does not have a bead, as the back of the flower is showing.

Thread up with the thin no 15 ribbon and form the leaves and calyx at the base of the buds and flowers in detached chain/lazy daisy or fly stitch.

Finally, thread up with the Black Berry thread and add more stab stitches on the leaves and calyx and form the short stems to add some interesting shadows.

Pimpernel

Anagallis arvensis

Scarlet pimpernel or shepherd's clock is a European native widely regarded as weed, but now found throughout the world. A hardy, annual herb that flowers in spring and summer, it prefers a sunny position and dry and sandy soil and will not grow in the shade. Single five-petalled flowers are borne on smooth, low, rambling stems in spring and summer. They only open when the sun shines and close on dull, overcast days, hence the name "poor man's weather glass"! Flowers are red-orange with some blue varieties also found in the wild. Once regarded as a medicinal herb and used for depression and epilepsy, there is little evidence to support its effectiveness and it is no longer recommended for internal use. The genus name Anagallis *is from the Greek word* Anagelao *meaning* to laugh, *which may explain why ancient Greeks used the herb for depression.*

CHAMELEON THREADS
Pure silk: Green Olives no 97 Use 1 strand of thread unless otherwise specified
DI VAN NIEKERK'S RIBBONS
Silk: 2-mm no 93, no 53 and no 29
STITCHES
Stem stitch – whipped, chain stitch – whipped, French knot, detached chain/lazy daisy, ribbon stitch, straight/stab stitch
NEEDLES
Use the no 9 or no 10 crewel for one strand of thread and the no 22 or 24 for the 2-mm ribbon

Hint: *Embroider this interesting flower to add a special touch to a beautiful scrapbook page, or for card-making. Embroider on a cotton or organza background, stretch and mount before gluing to the page or card using acid-free glue.*

Thread up with the green thread and work the rambling stems using whipped stem- or back stitch. Stem stitch is a better choice for tightly curled stems, as back stitch does not curve well. Keep the needle and thread on the outside (widest part) of the curve each time to form soft, rounded curves. Keep the stitches small and pull the thread taut before making the next stitch. Whip the stem by inserting the needle under and over the stitches each time. Pull the thread taut for a neat finish.

Now work the petals. Thread up with the orange ribbon (no 93) and make a French knot (one or two wraps) for each petal. Change to the yellow ribbon and form the yellow centre with a French knot (one wrap). Change to the green thread and use a straight/stab stitch to form the dark green sepals that are visible between the orange petals.

Form the buds in the same ribbon and detached chain/lazy daisy or ribbon stitch.

Form the leaves. Change to the thin green ribbon (no 29) and use small detached chain/lazy daisy stitches to make the egg-shaped leaves. Complete by adding the green calyx at the base of each bud with small, short ribbon stitches.

Rose

Genus Rosa

The genus Rosa *has some 150 species and has been around for 35 million years. Probably the best known and most admired flower in the world, roses have always been valued for their beauty. Fragrant rose petals have been used for centuries to make aromatic oils. Rich in Vitamin C, rose-petal water was used in China for stomach ailments. Roses were also the most revered flowers in Egypt, and Cleopatra used rose petals daily in her bedding and on her floors. About 3 000 years ago it was probably gardeners in China who started cultivating garden roses and these were introduced to Europe in the late eighteenth century. Depicted here are one of the popular old roses, with large, open flowers, prominent stamens and masses of pollen.*

Hint: *Embroider this life-like rose on velvet or Dupion silk to cover jewellery or trinket boxes. Embroider on cushions or hair bands. Use the ribbon techniques to embellish a wedding dress or embroider on a pink organza fabric and once complete, cut the excess fabric away and turn in the seams so they are hidden behind the rose. Apply a press stud or pin and use as a stunning accessory on a jacket, jersey or hat.*

CHAMELEON THREADS
Pure silk: Green Olives no 97, Rustic Brick no 66, Knysna Forest no 3, Rose no 64, Goldrush no 37 Use 1 strand of thread unless otherwise specified
DI VAN NIEKERK'S RIBBONS
Silk: 2-mm no 29 for the stems (or use a small piece of soft green wool) no 36, 13-mm no 45 and no 46
STITCHES
Couching, whipped stem or chain stitch, straight/stab stitch, back stitch, French knot, ribbon stitch, long and short stitch, buttonhole stitch, satin stitch, loop stitch, pistil stitch
NEEDLES
Use the no 9 or no 10 crewel for one strand of thread Use the no 22 or no 24 for the 2-mm ribbon and no 18 for the 13-mm ribbon Use a large no 13 tapestry needle to hold the loop stitches in shape

Start with the stems. Use the wool or no 29 2-mm silk ribbon and couch in place with the pale green thread every centimetre or so. Work over the leaves and pink petals of the rose on the right and insert the needle to the back in the centre of the rose. Bring the needle out in the centre of the rose on the left and proceed down the stem, couching the stem in place as before.

Whip the main stem by inserting the needle under and over the couched stem and end off at the base by taking the needle to the back again.

Work the thin stems growing from the main stem in the brown thread and whipped stem or chain stitch. The very short stems from the leaves are made in straight stitch.

Work the leaves next. Outline the serrated edges in tiny back stitches and the brown thread to create shadows. Thread up with the dark green thread and use long and short buttonhole stitch to make the leaves (see Wood poppy on page 28).

Use the brown thread and satin stitch to highlight one side of some leaves in brown to create an interesting effect. Use the same thread and stab stitch to add a few thorns along the thicker (main) stem.

Form the larger green calyx on the V of the thick green stems in ribbon stitch and 2-mm ribbon no 36

Start with the rose on the right. Thread up with 13-mm ribbon no 45 and form the outer petals first. Make the first circle of petals alternating with loose, puffed ribbon stitch and loose, puffed straight stitch. Insert a large tapestry needle or kebab stick under the straight stitch and lift the stitch up to form a loose petal. Thread up with the pink thread and use tiny stab stitches at the base of each stitch and along the edge to stabilize the stitch. Work with a gentle tension so the ribbon is not flattened.

Make the second inner circle of petals. Use the same method, keeping stitches loose and puffed. Make one or two petals in loop stitch for an attractive variation. At this stage the rose does not look much like a rose at all. It is only once the centre is added in the next step that it all comes together. Use the Rose thread as before to stabilize the ribbon stitches. Use the same thread and tiny stab stitches at the back of the work to secure the looped stitches. This prevents the stitches from being pulled out of shape as the next stitch is made.

Hint: *Always leave the ribbon on top of the work before securing the stitches at the back.*

Change to the 13-mm ribbon no 46 and make one or two coral petals in front of the inner circle of petals for an interesting play with colour.

Use the pink thread and stab stitch to tuck in any petals that are too large on the outer edge of the rose. Catch the ribbon underneath the fold so the stitch is invisible.

Thread up with the golden thread and make a cluster of French knots (2 wraps) inbetween the centre petals to make the golden yellow stamens Use the same thread and pistil stitch to make the longer stamens. Change to the brown thread and add a few darker French knots and pistil stitch to form the shadows. Don't work any stitches on top of the front petals to keep them soft and elevated.

Form the rose on the left in the same way. Thread up with 13-mm no 46 and form the outer circle of petals. Change to no 45 and form the inner circle as before. Add the golden stamens and brown shadows, allowing some petals in front to be soft and loose.

Butterfly

Butterfly order Lepidoptera

There are about 150 000 butterfly and moth species worldwide, both from the order Lepidoptera. *The beautiful Brenton Blue butterfly depicted here is severely endangered and one of the rarest butterflies in the world. It occurs only in a small patch of fynbos at a coastal town, Brenton-on-Sea, near Knysna in South Africa. Its survival depends on the presence of a specific host plant on which its larvae feed. All development in the butterfly's breeding area has been stopped and it has been turned into a unique reserve.*

Hint: *Pre-printed full-colour panels with the different embroidery shapes are available in from our website (www.dicraft.co.za). It is certainly is much easier to embroider on a colour-printed image than a line-tracing.*

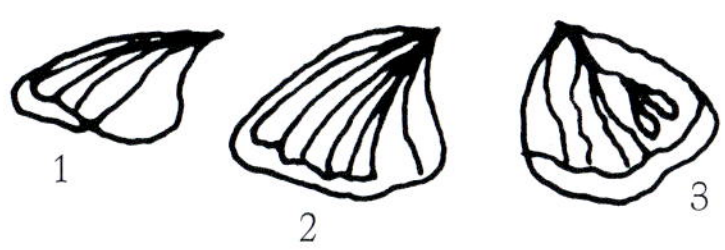

REQUIREMENTS
20 x 20 cm soft white polycotton or cotton Sharp HB or 2B pencil #30 wire-white or green from cake decorating shop Mill Hill petite glass beads no 42014, no 42041 Mill Hill beads no 40161 Fray Stop or anti-fray agent Kreinik blending filament no 32 Pearl
CHAMELEON THREADS
Pure silk: Arctic Blue no 5, Gold Nugget no 2 Use 1 strand of thread unless otherwise specified
RAJMAHAL ART SILK
no 226 Gothic Grey, no 25 Lagerfeld Ink or no 29 Charcoal
STITCHES
Couching, buttonhole/ blanket stitch, long and short stitch, straight /stab stitch, stem stitch, French knots, folded straight stitch, back stitch
NEEDLES
Use the no 9 or no 10 crewel needle for one strand of thread and the no 10 crewel for beading

Start with the wings. If you don't have a printed shape, trace the three wing shapes in the centre of the white fabric with a sharp HB or 2B pencil. Trace all the direction lines and detail as neatly as possible to ensure a good finish. Insert the fabric in a 15 cm (6 in) hoop. Pull the fabric taut as a drum and tighten the hoop. Roll up the corners and pin or tack out of the way so they don't hinder you as you work.

Use the #30 wire for the wings. First strip the plastic coating off the wire by holding the wire on a towel or dishcloth. Use the outer blunt edge of the old pair of scissors and run the scissors over the wire to strip the coating (see page 21). This way the wire is finer and not too thick for the delicate wings.

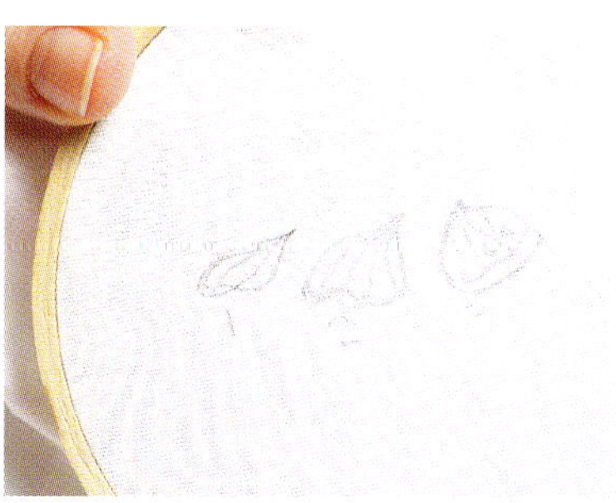

Insert 2 or 3 cm of the wire to the back of the work on the sharp point of each wing. Tape the wire in place with masking tape so it is out of the way and won't be caught on your threads as you embroider.

Couch the wire in place every 3-mm or so with the grey thread. To form a neat edge, angle the needle close to the wire, over, and back into the same hole again. Insert the wire to the back again and tape in place as before.

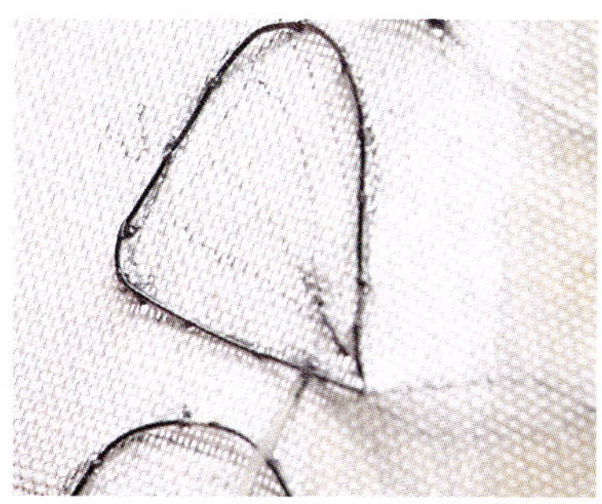

Hint: *Start with a knot at the long end, but ensure the knot is never along the edge of the shape. Always start a short distance inside the wing and make a few running stitches to reach the outer*

edge again (the running stitches will be covered with stitches later) This way the knot is not cut by mistake when the shape is cut out at a later stage.

Use buttonhole stitch to cover the wire (see buttonhole stitch over wire page 153) Take the needle to the back before inserting it through the loop each time. Angle the needle under the wire for a neat edge.

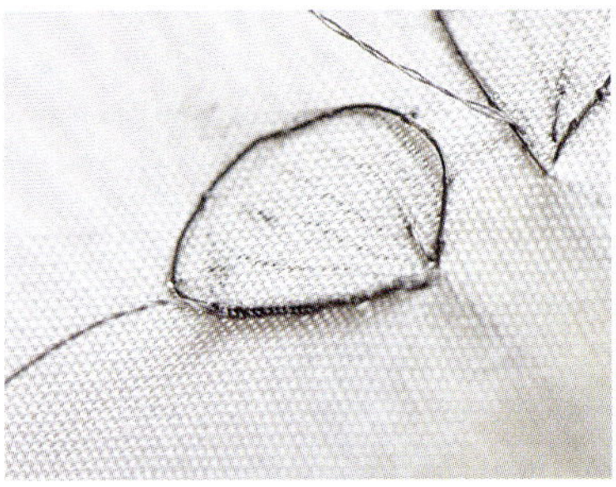

Form the veins in the same thread and stem or straight stitch. Change to the blue thread and fill in the blue scales in long and short stitch. Start at the tip and work outwards, fanning the stitches towards the top and bottom edge of the wings. Change to the light gold thread and fill in the golden scales the same way. For a frilly edge on wing 3, use blanket stitch to form the curved gold line. Change to the blending filament and add a few highlights on top of the blue in short straight stitch. Use the blue thread to add 3 denim blue beads on top of wing 3.

Work on the main design. Thread up with the black thread and form the head and thorax in French knots (one or two wraps) made close together. Add a white bead on top for the eye. Add a row of black beads, one by one in a row to form the slender abdomen ending with a small French knot. The legs are made in folded straight stitch and the two knobbed antennae in back stitch. Add one black bead at each tip. Use 3 or 4 anchoring stitches to secure the beads.

Cut out the wings. Remove the tape and apply an anti-fray agent along the edge. Cut close to the edge with small sharp embroidery scissors. Be careful not to cut the stitches.

Make a small hole on the main design alongside the butterfly's body with the sharp point of your small embroidery scissors, or use a size 16 or 18 chenille needle.

Place wing 1 first and bend the wires at the back of the work, so they lie under wing 1. Secure the wire in place with small stab stitches in the blue, grey or gold thread. Cut off the excess wire trimming the raw edges. (Use the nail clippers or old scissors to trim the wire edges.) so they don't catch on your threads as you work.

Hint: *To protect your threads, use a small piece of masking tape over the raw edges until the design has been completed.*

Place wing 2 in the same hole, attaching it in place as before. Do the same for wing 3, placing it so it overlaps wings 1 and 2.

Hint: *If the hole is too small, extend it very slightly or make another next to the previous hole.*

Attach the wires at the back as before. Use the grey thread and tiny stab stitches along the base of the wings and body on the right side to secure in place. Stitch over the wired edges, so the stab stitches blend in well. Leave the outer, rounded edges free so the wings are raised off the design. Bend the wings into a pleasing shape.

PANEL EIGHT

Honeysuckle

Beetle

Hawk moth

Hawk moth

Honeysuckle

Lonicera periclymenum

Woodbine or English honeysuckle is a hardy, easy to grow, fragrant, vigorous and compact climber reaching a height of up to 7 metres. Will cover a trellis, garden wall or fence in no time at all. The lush purple-red buds unfold to reveal fragrant, creamy cartwheel-like flowers, followed by red berries after the flowering season. In constant bloom from mid-summer to autumn, honeysuckle shrub species also make good border and container plants. They like full sun to semi-shade and well drained, fertile soil. The colourful, fragrant flowers attract butterflies, moths and hummingbirds.

Hint: *A spray of honeysuckle will look good on a handbag or trinket-box cover. Embroider on the borders of a quilt or in the corners of a cushion. Embellish a jersey collar or the hem of a guest towel. Embroider on sheer organza or cross-stitch fabric, stretch, and glue to your scrapbook page or card.*

REQUIREMENTS
Mill Hill glass seed beads no 02066 20 x 20 cm soft white polycotton or cotton Sharp 2B or HB pencil Spray Stop or any good anti-fray agent
CHAMELEON THREADS
Pure silk: Green Olives no 97, Emerald no 101, Knysna Forest no 3, Gold Nugget no 3 Use 1 strand of thread unless otherwise specified
DI VAN NIEKERK'S RIBBONS
Silk: 4-mm no 109, no 90 and no 112
STITCHES
Long and short buttonhole stitch, detached chain/lazy daisy, long and short stitch, satin stitch, fly stitch, straight/stab stitch, twisted straight stitch, ribbon stitch, pistil stitch
NEEDLES
Use the fine no 9 or no 10 crewel for the threads and beads Use a no 20 or no 22 chenille for the 4-mm ribbon

The leaves are made separately, then attached to the background. Use a sharp HB or 2B pencil and trace the eight leaves in the centre of the white fabric block. Leave a centimetre gap between the shapes. Trace all the detail on the leaves.

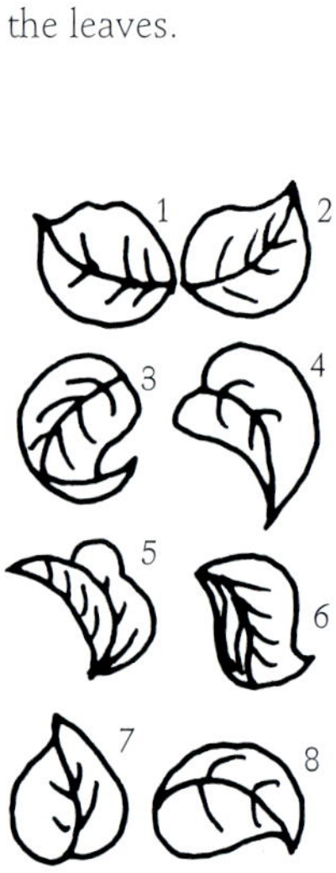

Number each leaf at the side of the shape to guide you later. Insert in a 15 cm (6 in) hoop. Roll up the corners and pin them out of the way.

Hint: *Trace the beetle on page 76 on the same fabric block, as this will save time later.*

There is no need for wire around the edge of these leaves, as they do not need to be bent into shape. Embroider the darker leaves 4 to 8 first. Thread up with the emerald green thread and use a long and short buttonhole stitch to form a neat edge. Start at the pointed tip with a detached chain and continue down the one half of the leaf in long and short buttonhole stitch. Start at the sharp tip again and outline the other half as before. Fill in the leaf with long and short or satin stitch and insert the needle along the central vein each time. Use the same thread and stitch along the darker folded sections of leaves 1 to 3 as before.

Hint: *Remember to slant the stitch towards the base of the leaf all the time for a natural finish.*

Change to the lighter green thread and complete the lighter sections on leaves in the same way. Thread up with the golden thread and use fly stitch and straight/stab stitch to form the veins. Set aside until the flowers are completed.

Work on the main design. Thread up with the pink silk ribbon and use a twisted straight stitch to form the pink stems. Work from the top downwards and stitch over the leaves and flowers, as these will be added on top later. Thread up with the light green thread and couch the ribbon in place with tiny stab stitches every centimetre or so. Use the pink ribbon again and whip the thicker stems by inserting the needle under and over the couched stem. Form the shorter twirled side stems in the same pink ribbon and twisted straight stitch for the thin stems and long detached chain/lazy daisy for others. Add a few straight stitches overlapping each other for more texture.

Change to the burnt orange ribbon and form the orange petals on the stem in ribbon stitch, forming one stitch on top of another to make a larger petal. Thread up with the cream ribbon and make the cream petals in ribbon stitch, some twisted to form a curved petal. Use a gentle tension and push the ribbon up as you insert the needle into the ribbon to form loose, puffed petals.

Thread up with the light green thread and use a pistil stitch to form the green stamens. To enlarge the anthers at the tip of the stalk, use a tiny detached chain/lazy daisy. Thread up with a green bead and attach one bead for each cluster of petals.

Cut out the leaves. (See camellia leaves in Panel 4 page 44.) Attach each leaf on top of the honeysuckle flowers, placing the leaves to match the shapes and sizes of the leaves on the main design. Use the dark green thread and secure the leaves on the design with tiny stab stitches along the rounded base. Stitch along edges and tips of a few leaves and leave others unstitched along the tips for an interesting variation. Thread up with a green bead and attach one at a time with four or five stitches. Form a cluster of five or six beads at the base of the leaves.

Hint: *Wait until the beetle has been completed as detailed in the next section before cutting out the leaf shapes and do them all at the same time before attaching to the main embroidery.*

Beetle

Order Coleoptera

Coleoptera *comes from the Greek words* koleos *meaning* sheath *or* shield, *and* ptera *meaning* wing. *Beetles are the largest order in the animal kingdom, with over 350 000 species. Dung beetles (the well-known scarab beetle being one of them) play a valuable role in improving soil structure. Some beetles are brightly coloured, some are green, others are yellow and black imitating wasps, and some are black to suit their nocturnal habits.*

Hint: *Use this beetle on a scrapbook page or card to add a special touch (see the Termites in Panel 5, page 55 for more ideas).*

REQUIREMENTS
20x 20 cm soft white polycotton or cotton Sharp HB or 2B pencil Fray stop or any clear-drying anti-fray agent
CHAMELEON THREADS
Pure silk: Charcoal no 15, Rustic Brick no 66 Use 1 strand of thread unless otherwise specified
RAJMAHAL ART SILK
Lagerfeld Ink no 25 or Charcoal no 29
STITCHES
Stem stitch, satin stitch, pistil stitch, straight/stab stitch, straight stitch – folded
NEEDLES
Use a no 9 or no 10 crewel needle for the beetle

Make the body of the beetle first. If you have not already done so, trace the beetle's body on the white fabric. Use a sharp HB or 2B pencil. Place the fabric in a 15 cm (6 in) hoop.

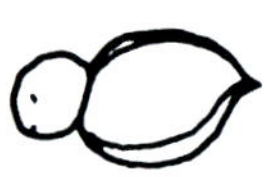

Thread up with 2 strands of Rajmahal Art Silk thread and outline the head and body in tiny stem stitch. Fill the head in satin stitch working from the neck towards the mouth.

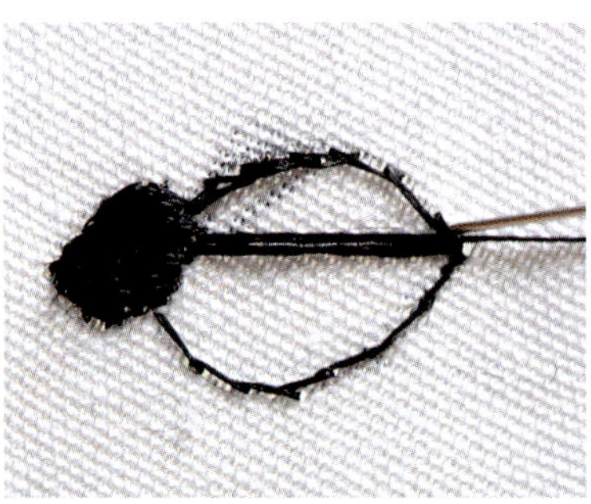

Hint: *Stitch over the black outline stitch so the satin stitch is padded.*

The body is made the same way. Work from the head towards the sharp tip of the abdomen. Change to the rustic brown thread and add a few straight stitches on top to form the brown streaks. Thread up with the Rajmahal art silk and outline the shape once again with two or three rows of stem stitch made close together.

Use Fray Stop or anti fray agent along the edge and cut out as you did for the honeysuckle leaves in the previous section. Attach the shape to the background in the Charcoal thread using tiny stab stitches.

Hint: *Pinch the shape before attaching it to the design to make a dome shaped body that is raised off the design.*

Thread up with one strand of Rajmahal Art Silk thread and form an outline along the body and head in stem stitch. Form the legs in stab stitch for the short top section and pistil stitch for the longer straight lines. The antennae are worked in pistil stitch or folded straight stitch. Work from the head outwards.

Hawk moth

Order Lepidoptera

Moths are closely related to butterflies and belong to the same order. Hawk moths are among the most beautiful in the world and, like most moths, are active at night. They are fast flyers, some reaching a speed of more than 45 km per hour. Spread world-wide, there are about nine hundred known species of hawk moth. Most of them feed on flower nectar. Their forewings are twice or three times larger than their hindwings. They have large heads and eyes with a large tapered abdomen. The bee-hawk moth looks and acts like a bumblebee. Its yellow and black body and transparent wings often fool birds and other predators that it is a bumblebee.

Hint: *Use this technique to add a special touch to clothing, scrapbook pages, curtains, handbags, quilts, cushions and many other projects. Instead of embroidering the body directly on the design as shown here, use water-soluble fabric as for the Oxalis (page 20), and glue or stitch the body in place. The wings are made as below and attached with thread for fabric backgrounds and glue for paper.*

REQUIREMENTS
Sharp 2B or 3B pencil or pen with water-soluble ink 3 x 3 cm medium-weight iron-on interfacing 20 x 20 cm water-soluble fabric Water-soluble multipurpose glue stick (similar to the ones used at school)
CHAMELEON THREADS
Pure silk: Egg Yolk no 28, Velvet Brown no 111 Stranded cotton: Baked Earth no 7 Use 1 strand of thread unless otherwise specified
RAJMAHAL ART SILK
Lagerfeld Ink no 25 or Charcoal no 29
DI VAN NIEKERK'S RIBBONS
Organza 15-mm no 124
STITCHES
Stem stitch or split stitch, satin stitch, straight/ stab stitch, blanket/buttonhole stitch
NEEDLES
Use a no 9 or no 10 crewel needle

Moth's wings for tracing:

Note: *The two large and two small wings are traced onto interfacing. The interfacing shapes are ironed onto the organza ribbon, cut out and then applied to the design – a form of free-standing appliqué. The organza has a lovely shine that results in a life-like finish.*

Trace the shapes on the smooth non-fusible side (not on the shiny or rough side) of the interfacing with all the detail. These shapes are ironed onto the organza ribbon to prevent fraying and to stabilize the wings. Use a soft, sharp 2B or 3B pencil or pen with water-soluble ink, and trace the shapes as neatly as possible.

Cut out the interfacing shapes a millimetre from the edge. Don't cut on the pencil line. To prevent fraying, you will only cut along the pencil line once the interfacing has been ironed onto the ribbon.

Place the length of the organza ribbon on the ironing board and press each interfacing wing onto the ribbon so the heat bonds it well. Use a medium setting with the steam off and place the wings shiny or rough side down on the ribbon. Be careful not to scorch the ribbon. Check that the shapes are attached to the ribbon and that the shapes do not lift at the edges.

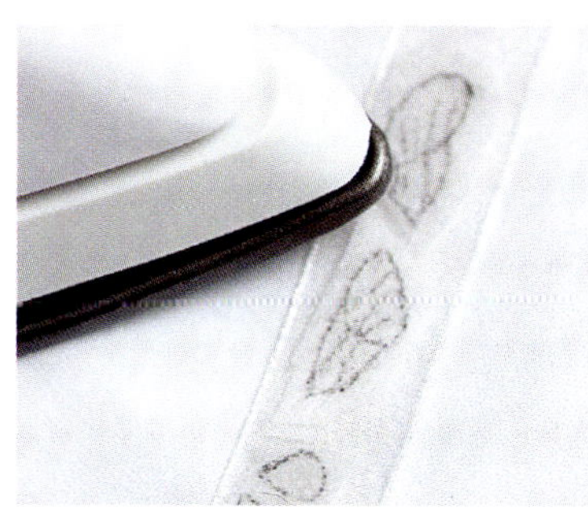

Cut out each shape along the pencil line as neatly as possible with small, sharp embroidery scissors.

Insert the water-soluble fabric in a 15 cm (6 in) hoop. Place the four shapes, ribbon-side up on the water-soluble fabric. Leave a 1 cm space between the shapes. Use a water-soluble multipurpose glue stick (similar to the ones used at school) to lightly glue the shapes to the water-soluble fabric.

Hint: *If too much glue is used, it dissolves the water-soluble fabric. Simply lift the shape and place elsewhere on the fabric.*

Thread up with the stranded cotton no 7 thread. Start at the narrowed base with a knot. Using blanket stitch along the edge, work anti-clockwise (clockwise if you are left-handed) around the shape. End off with a few back stitches on the base. Do the same for all four wings.

Hint: *Start with a knot at the long end, but ensure the knot is never along the edge of the shape. Always start a short distance inside the wing and make a running stitch to reach the outer edge again. This way the knot is not visible when the shape is attached to the design.*

Fill in the wings with the same thread, using long and short stitch or stem stitch filling. Leave small patches of the organza uncovered for an authentic finish. Change to the black thread and form a row of blanket stitches about 2 mm inside the rounded edge of the large wings to complete the shapes.

Cut out the shapes leaving a 5-mm (¼ in) edge of water soluble fabric. Place shapes in a bowl of water for one minute. Remove and allow the shapes to dry on a towel or dish-cloth.

Hint: *By leaving the shapes in the water only for a minute, the shapes are sticky and have more body. Once the shapes are dry, the wings are bent and retain their shape. Every now and then, while they are drying, move the wings so they don't stick to the towel or dishcloth.*

Work the body and antennae of the large moth. Use the black thread and outline the head in tiny stem or split stitch, embroider the antennae in stem stitch and the black stripes on the abdomen in straight stitch and satin stitch. Change to the velvet brown thread and fill in the head and thorax in satin stitch. The brown stripes on the abdomen are straight stitch. Add the yellow stripes in the same way.

Do the same for the small moth. Use the same threads and stitches to form the body and antennae. Use the velvet brown thread and tiny stab stitches along the base of the wings to attach alongside the body. Add a few tiny stitches along the sides to stabilize, allowing the rounded outer edges to be free.

PANEL NINE

Leucadendrons

Leucadendron xanthoconus

Common names: Sickle-leaf conebush, knoppiesbos, geelbos

Xanthoconus *is a Greek word meaning* yellow-coned, *an apt description for this plant. Up to 2 metres tall, this much-loved conebush from the* Proteaceae *family grows in sandy soils at sea level and up to 670 metres above sea level. It has soft, curved, narrow, and tapered bracts (leaves) that are bright yellow. The young leaves have delicate silver hairs at the tip of the branches, but as they age they grow to be hairless. A widespread shrub and popular garden plant, it flowers in spring.*

Hint: *Use this technique to add a special touch to a beautiful trinket box and on quilts or wall hangings. These raised and colourful flowers will be a beautiful focal point on any jersey or cushion.*

REQUIREMENTS
70 cm brown wool for the stems (chenille or bouclé works well) 20x 20 cm soft white polycotton or cotton Sharp HB or 2B pencil
CHAMELEON THREADS
Pure silk: Gold Nugget no 2, Gold Nugget no 3 Knysna Forest no 3 Stranded cotton: Baked Earth no 7 Use 1 strand of thread unless otherwise specified
DI VAN NIEKERK'S RIBBONS
Silk: 4-mm no 99
STITCHES
French knot, running stitch, couching, stab stitch, ribbon stitch, ribbon stitch – twisted, straight/stab stitch
NEEDLES
Use a no 8 or no 9 crewel for two strands of thread and no 9 or no 10 crewel for one strand of thread Use a no 20 or no 22 chenille for the 4-mm silk ribbon

Trace the four circles below in the centre of the white fabric. Trace in all the detail to guide you as you stitch. Remember to trace the outer dotted lines around the circles as these will be the gathering lines later. Insert in a 15 cm (6 in) hoop.

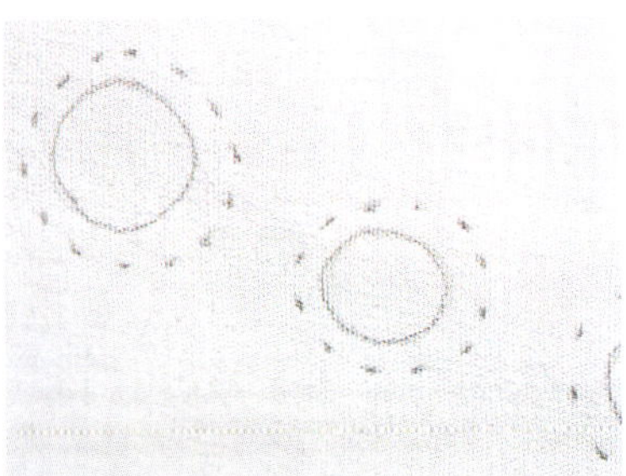

Use two strands of thread. Embroider the four circular cones alternating between the light and darker gold thread along the lower section on the circle. Use French knots (one wrap) and make the knots close together. Change to the green thread and add a few French knots in the top section of the circle. Change to the brown thread and add knots between the yellow and green stitches to form the dark shadows. End off the thread at the back.

Use the brown thread and make a knot at the long end. Form a circle of running stitches along the dotted line, leaving the length of thread hanging. Start with a new thread for each circle. Cut out the circles 3 mm away from the running stitch, taking care not to cut the thread.

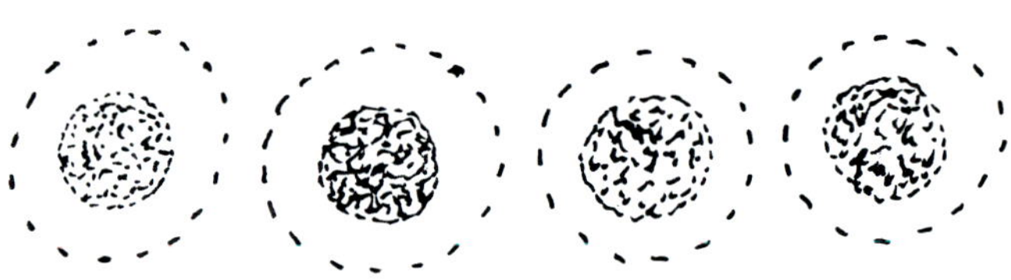

Pull the thread to gather the seam to the back. Use the same thread to anchor the seams to the wrong side of the circle. Set aside until later.

Form the stems. Lay the wool on top of the design and couch in place with the brown thread.

Hint: *There is no need to insert the wool in a needle. The wool stems look more realistic with the raw edge showing at the base of the stems.*

Start at the bottom of the panel, couch the wool at the raw edge and proceed up the length of the stem, couching in place every centimetre (½ in) or so. Stitch over the flowers and leaves, ending on top of the circular yellow/green cones. The flowers and leaves will be added on top later. Repeat for the other stems.

Attach the circular cones on top of the sampler, covering the raw ends of the stem. Use the brown thread and tiny stab stitches to secure in place.

Thread up with the yellow ribbon and work the bracts at the back of the circular cones with loose, puffed ribbon stitch, twisting some of the stitches for an interesting effect. Start under the cone and work outwards. Form the yellow bracts along the side and on then on top of the cones in the same way.

Hint: *When stitching through the cone, use a needle grabber (a round piece of rubber sheeting) or small pair of pliers to gently pull the needle through to the back of the work.*

Thread up with the brown thread and add straight/stab stitches at the tips of the bracts to stabilize the ribbon and to create a life-like flower.

Hint: *Use the same wool, thread, stitch and method to form the stems of all the leucadendrons in the panel as this will save time later. Stitch over the flowers and leaves as before.*

Leucadendron sheilae

Common name: Lokenberg conebush

Endemic to South Africa Leucadendron sheilae *was named after Sheila, the wife of Dr Ion Williams, who assisted him with his valuable research into South Africa's approximately 80 leucadendron species. Dr Williams received world acclaim and brought international recognition for Hermanus in the Overberg region of the Western Cape.* L. sheilae *has the typical leathery bracts (leaves) and central cone of this genus.*

Hint: *Use this technique to adorn a trinket-box cover. This flower is ideal for quilts, wall-hangings, jerseys and cushions.*

CHAMELEON THREADS
Pure silk: Scottish Heather no 68, Velvet Brown no 111, Charcoal no 15, Egg Yolk no 28 Stranded cotton: Baked Earth no 7 Use 1 strand of thread unless otherwise specified
DI VAN NIEKERK'S RIBBONS
Silk: 7-mm no 109; Organza: 7-mm no 14
STITCHES
Ribbon stitch, ribbon stitch – folded, ribbon stitch – twisted, stab stitch, French knot, turkey stitch, stem stitch
NEEDLES
Use a no 8 or no 9 crewel for two strands of thread and a no 9 or no 10 crewel for one strand Use the no 18 chenille for the silk and organza ribbon

If you haven't worked the stems when doing those of the previous leucadendron, do them now (see page 81).

Work the yellow bracts in the cream ribbon using loose, puffed ribbon stitch. Some folded bracts are formed in folded ribbon stitch, others are made in twisted ribbon stitch. Keep a loose tension throughout.

Thread up with the velvet brown thread and make a few stab stitches at the tips of the bracts, then small French knots (one wrap) to add more texture. Use the baked earth brown thread and add further dark shadows alongside the bracts in the same stab stitch. Finally, use the grey thread and stab stitch to fill in the grey points on each bract.

Work the centre cone of the leucadendrons on top of the ribbon bracts. Thread up with the black thread and work the half-moon shapes in French knots (two wraps) Change to two strands of the yellow thread and use turkey stitch to complete the top half of the cone. Cut some of the loops (and fluff gently) and leave other stitches looped for an interesting texture.

Complete the grey leaves in the organza ribbon and folded ribbon stitch. Change to the grey thread and use a few stab stitches on the tips to secure the ribbon and to add texture. Change to the baked earth brown thread and use a stem stitch alongside one or two of the ribbon leaves to add the shadows.

Leucadendron eucalyptifolium

Common names: Gum-leaf conebush, tall yellowbush, groot-geelbos, geelbos

A vigorous grower reaching heights of up to 5 metres, this magnificent Leucadendron flowers in winter and early spring bearing masses of small flowerheads with long, narrow, bright yellow bracts surrounding the creamy-yellow cones. Named for its long, narrow, fragrant, eucalyptus-like leaves that form a ring beneath the flower, although these do not differ much from the leaves of other Leucadendrons. It likes sandy soil, is easy to grow and is becoming a popular cut flower.

Hint: *Use this technique to add a special touch to a beautiful trinket box and for a super feature on quilts, fire screens, footstools and wall hangings.*

Note: *The stem was couched together with those of the other leucadendrons. If you have not done so yet,* *see page 81* *and do so now.*

REQUIREMENTS

20x 20 cm soft white polycotton or cotton
Sharp HB or 2B pencil
#28 green or white wire from cake decorating shops
Fray Stop or any good anti-fray agent
Small piece of toy filling

CHAMELEON THREADS

Pure silk: Tropical Green no 3, Granite no 105, Gold Nugget no 2 Gold Nugget no 3, Knysna Forest no 3, Charcoal no 15
Stranded cotton: Baked Earth no 7
Use 1 strand of thread unless otherwise specified

DI VAN NIEKERK'S RIBBONS

Silk: 13-mm no 36, 4-mm no 82

STITCHES

Couching, ribbon stitch, straight /stab stitch, French knot, stem stitch, buttonhole stitch, buttonhole – long and short, long and short stitch, back stitch, detached chain/lazy daisy, blanket stitch, pistil stitch

NEEDLES

Use a no 8 or no 9 crewel for two strands of thread and no 9 or 10 crewel for one strand of thread; use a no 18 chenille for the 13-mm silk ribbon, no 20 to 22 for the 4-mm ribbon

Work the large green leaves in green silk ribbon and use one ribbon stitch for each leaf. Work from the centre outwards stitching over the yellow bracts as these will be added on top later. Work over the yellow bract of the *Leucadendron sheilae*, then change to the yellow ribbon used for *L. sheilae* earlier and make a ribbon stitch on top of the green leaf.

Change to the green thread and use tiny stab stitches (every centimetre or so) along the sides of the leaf to secure the ribbon to the design. Use the same stab stitch and embroider on the tip of the leaf as well. Three or four stab stitches are sufficient.

Hint: *Stitch under the folded edge so the stitches are invisible – this way the ribbon curls up nicely.*

Change to the Granite thread and add dark shadows on the tips in stab stitch and French knots (two wraps.) Use the same thread and a stem stitch on the design, close to the curled edge to add the shadows.

Make the yellow bracts. Trace the shapes on the next page in the centre of the small fabric block. Number each bract alongside the shape (there

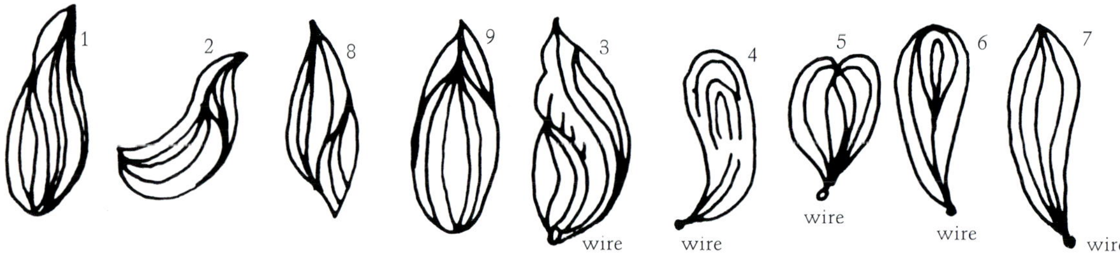

are 9 leaves). Use a sharp HB or 2B pencil and draw in the detail of the leaves as direction lines to guide you as you embroider each shape. Insert in a 15 cm (6 in) hoop. Pull the fabric taut and tighten the hoop. Roll up the four corners and pin or tack out of the way so they don't hinder you as you work.

Only bracts 3, 4, 5, 6, and 7 have a wired edge as they are raised or folded. Make a small hole with the no 16 chenille needle at the base of bract no 3. Insert 2 cm of the #28 wire in the hole and bend the length of wire in shape to follow the edge of the bract Insert it back in the hole again. Leave a 2 cm tail and cut off the excess wire with a pair of nail clippers or old scissors. Secure the raw ends of the wire to the back of the work with a piece of masking tape ensuring the tape is not covering any area that needs to be stitched. Repeat for bracts 4 to 7.

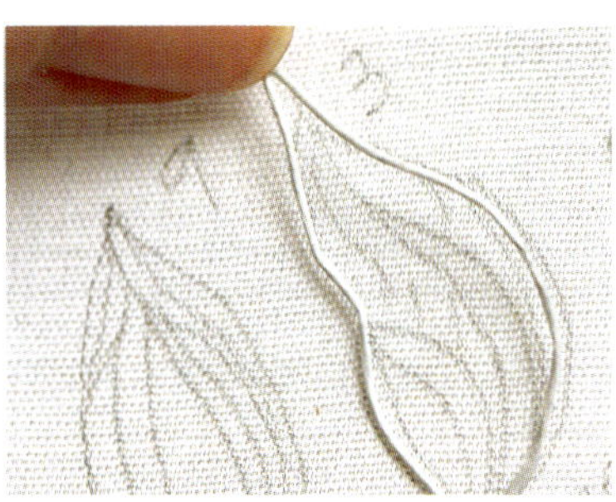

Hint: *When working the shapes, start with a knot and remember to always start by inserting the needle, about 4-mm away from the edge inside the leaf shape. Make small running stitches to the edge and continue as usual. The running stitches will be covered with long and short stitch in the next step. This way the knot will not be severed when the shape is cut out later.*

Couch the wire in place every 4 mm or so with the light gold thread.

Cover the wire with buttonhole stitch in the brown thread along the edge of one half of the wired bracts.

Change to the green thread and complete the opposite edge in the same stitch. This way one side of the bract is brown and the other green. Repeat for all five wired bracts.

Outline the remaining four bracts that do not have a wired edge. The same buttonhole stitch is used for a neat cutting edge. Thread up with the brown thread and work long and short buttonhole stitch to form a neat edge along one side of each bract. Repeat along the other side using the same brown thread.

Use the darker gold thread and long and short stitch to fill in the tip and edges of all nine yellow bracts. Start at the tip and work down towards the base of the bract, following the direction lines on the shape. Stitch along the outer edge too.

Hint: *Keep the stitches quite neat at the back of the tips and the sides of the bracts as they will be folded back once attached to the design. Remember to start and end in the centre or along the base of the leaf so there aren't any knots showing once the tip and edge are folded back.*

Change to the lighter gold thread and fill in the centre of the shape working downwards towards the base. Use the brown thread and add a few dark lines in straight stitch, at the base and tip of each leaf.

Change to the green thread and add a few green straight/stab stitches on top of the golden ones to form a few green shadows.

Hint: *Follow the placement diagram below and as each bract is cut out, place it on the table in the correct position so the bracts are easily identified when you start to attach them to the design.*

Remove the tape from the wired bracts and apply the anti-fray agent along the edges and the embroidered section of each bract (first check that it dries clear). Cut out each bract a few mm away from the edge.

Once you are holding a shape in your hand, carefully cut away the fabric to the edge. Take care not to cut the wire on leaves 3 to 7 and angle the scissors so the bottom blade is under the shape for a neat edge. Take care not to cut your stitches. (If this does happen, use the anti-fray agent again or clear nail polish to stabilize the stitch.)

Work on the main design. Thread up with the brown thread and, following the placement guide, attach the unwired bracts using tiny stab stitches at the base of each bract. Attach one at a time in this sequence: 1, 2, 8 and 9. Work over the green cone in the centre – it will be worked later. Align the tip of each bract with the bract on the design (overlapping a few mm) and let the bracts overlap at the base and along the edges as on the design.

Attach the wired bracts in this sequence: 3, 4, 5, 6, and 7. Use a no 16 chenille needle or the sharp point of small embroidery scissors to make a small hole at the base of each bract, on top of the brown edge around the green cone. Insert the wires of each bract, bending them backwards at the back of the work, so the wires lie beneath the shape. Attach the wire to the back with the same thread and tiny stab stitches and trim the ends with an old pair of scissors or nail clippers to ensure there are no raw edges that may damage the threads later.

Slightly dampen bracts 1, 2, 8 and 9 with the anti-fray agent and bend each into a pleasing shape. Keep working at it until each bract is dry and retains its shape. Now shape the wired leaves. They needn't be dampened with the anti-fray agent, as the wire holds the shape. Fold the tips towards the centre of the flower and bend the wire to form the upturned end. Pinch bract 3 between your thumb and forefinge,r so both edges are turned upwards.

Make the green cone to form the centre of the flower. Trace the two shapes on off-cuts from the white fabric used for the bracts. Fill in all the detail, as this will guide you as you work. Cut out on the dotted line.

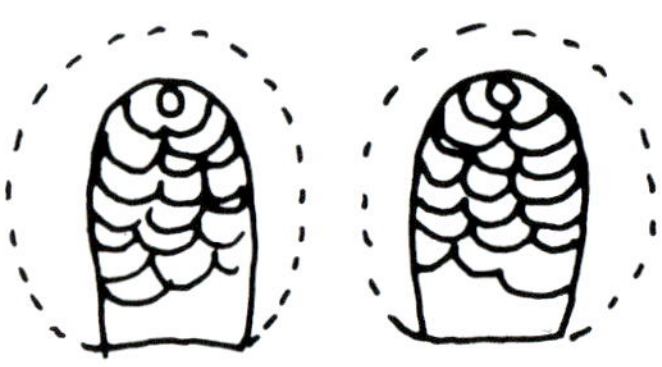

Place one shape, right side down against a sunny window or light box and trace the dark outer line of the shape. Place the shapes right sides together and pin in the centre. Use two strands of green thread and small back stitches to sew along the oval line you have just pencilled in, leaving the flat edges open so the shape can be turned inside out. Cut small slits in the seam every 3 mm or so and turn right side out with scissors with blunt points or small dowel or rounded stick. Carefully push the seam out to form a rounded edge. Use the same scissors or stick to hold the cone in place while you embroider it.

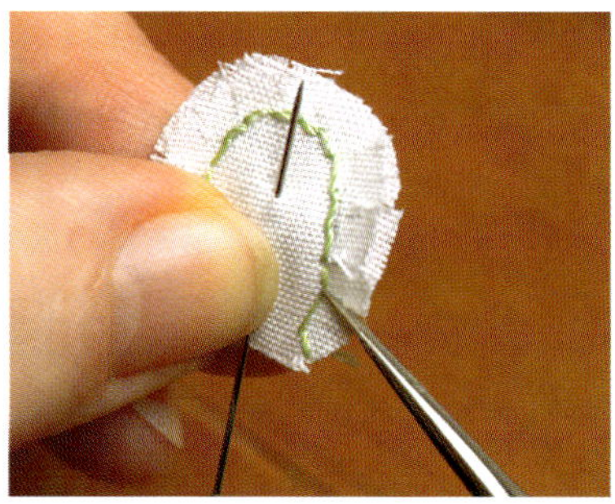

Thread up with the 4-mm green silk ribbon and make a small knot at the long end. Insert the needle inside the shape exiting at the curved tip of the cone. Form a detached chain/lazy daisy as your first stitch, then proceed with row after row of loose blanket stitch. Work around the shape and continue until the entire shape is covered with ribbon.

Hint: *Keep a gentle tension to form loose, frilly blanket stitches. End off by inserting the needle inside the cone and exit at the open base. Leave a tail and cut off the ribbon. Use the green thread to secure the tail of the ribbon to the flat base of the cone. Start with a knot again and proceed with the next row.*

Fill the cone with a small ball of shredded wadding or toy filling to form a compact, rounded cone. Thread up with the green thread with a knot at the long end, and insert the needle inside the open edge of the cone Secure the cone on top of the leaves with tiny stab stitches tucking the raw edges under the cone as you stitch. Work through all the layers so the cone is well secured. Stitch through the leaves, taking the needle to the back of the work before inserting it back to the front again. Note how the cone faces up towards the left.

Change to black thread and work the collar at the base of the cone in pistil stitch. One or two pistil stitches on each leaf is sufficient.

PANEL TEN

Hedgehog **English bluebells**

Hedgehog

Atelerix albiventrishas

The African Pygmy Hedgehog is found in the wild from Zambia to as far north as Sudan in dry habitats. It is a good swimmer and can climb trees to escape predators. It has short limbs with an oval-shaped body. Reaching 18 to 23 cm in length, it is covered with small brown or grey spines with cream tips and has a furry soft tummy. The female is slightly bigger than the male and they breed once or twice a year, with gestation lasting about 35 days. The young are born with their spines already in place, but covered in a membrane which shrivels and dries soon after birth. They have a life-span of 8 to 10 years. Being a nocturnal animal, the hedgehog feeds on insects, spiders and plants in the wild.

Hint: *A row of hedgehogs will look so cute on a little girl's dress. A great idea for inserting on quilt or cushion borders and along the hem of a guest towel or napkin. To use for card-making or scrapbooking, embroider on water-soluble fabric. Follow the method described for the ants on page 109. A row of hedgehogs hidden by long pieces of ribbon or wool is sure to add a touch of humour to any project!*

REQUIREMENTS
Piece of fluffy green wool or Norbillie fibre for green lawn in front and a matching green cotton or silk thread to couch in place
CHAMELEON THREADS
Pure silk: Velvet Brown no 111 Use 1 strand of thread throughout
RAJMAHAL ART SILK
No 25 Lagerfeld Ink or Charcoal no 29, Gothic Grey no 226 White no 96
STITCHES
Couching, straight/stab stitch, stem or split stitch, back stitch, French knot, stem stitch filling, long and short stitch
NEEDLES
Use a no 9 or no 10 (fine) crewel needle

Start with the grass. Lay the piece of wool or fibre along the bottom edge of the design and couch in place every 5 to 10 mm (¼ to ½ in) with a matching green thread.

Work the hedgehog. Thread up with the black thread and start under the eye. Make tiny vertical (upright) stab stitches to form the black shadows beneath the eye. Use even smaller stitches above the eye to make the dark "eyelashes".

Use tiny stem or split stitch to outline the outer oval and the inner oval of the eye in the same thread.

Form the little mouth in diagonal stab stitch. Outline the leg and toes in the same thread and stem or back stitch. Form the black spines (quills) in straight/stab stitch, leaving space in between to fill with grey, white and brown stitches.

Stitch over the green leaves, as these will be added on top later.

Change to the white thread and use two tiny stab stitches between the inner and outer ovals of the eye to form the white line. Use a small French knot (two wraps) in the very centre to complete the eye. Use the same white thread and outline the ear in tiny split or stem stitch.

Add a French knot (two wraps) in the centre of the ear. Form the white spines (quills) in straight /stab stitch as shown.

Change to the dark grey thread and use straight/stab stitch to form the grey spines (quills) alongside the black and white stitches on the body. Stitch over the leaves, as these will be added on top later.

Use stem stitch filling – rows of stem stitch made close together – to fill in the foot and toes. Fill in the nose in long and short stitch working from the tip towards the eye. Fan the stitches out towards the sides of the nose going back to fill in the gaps. Fill in the area beneath the mouth in the same way.

Hint: *To add further highlights on the body, use the white thread and straight/stab stitch on top of the brown and black quills.*

Change to the brown thread and fill in the remaining spaces between the spines. Use straight/stab stitch as before. Add the brown streaks on the nose, body and leg in straight/stab stitch to complete the hedgehog.

English bluebell

Hyacinthoides non-scripta

The flowering of the English bluebells is said to be a breathtaking sight for anyone fortunate enough to be in the UK in spring. With their strong yet graceful, curved stems and deep violet blue bell-shaped flowers they form a magnificent carpet of blue flowers in shady woodlands and reappear and proliferate year after year. The English bluebell is a hardy perennial, has a wonderful honey fragrance that attracts butterflies en masse and grows to a height of 30 or 40 cm (12 to 16 in). Loves shade or partial shade and is an ideal bulb to grow in moist, shady areas in the garden.

Hint: *A cluster of English bluebells is spectacular on a jersey, dress or handbag. The colour and texture of these beautiful flowers will enhance any garment, cushion or quilt. Follow these instructions and embroider directly on the fabric or knitted jersey. Or embroider on an organza or netting background and stretch and mount to make a beautiful card or scrapbook page.*

CHAMELEON THREADS
Pure silk: Knysna Forest no 3, Arctic Blue no 5, Use 1 strand of thread unless otherwise specified
DI VAN NIEKERK'S RIBBONS
Silk 2-mm no 16, 4-mm no 64, 7-mm no 15
STITCHES
Straight stitch – twisted, straight/stab stitch, couching, straight stitch – folded, ribbon stitch – folded, ribbon stitch – twisted, detached chain/lazy daisy, grab stitch
NEEDLES
Use the no 9 or no 10 (fine) crewel for one strand of thread Use the no 22 or no 24 chenille for the 2-mm ribbon, a no 20 or no 22 for the 4-mm ribbon and a no 18 or no 20 for the 7-mm ribbon

Work the stems first. Thread up with the 2-mm ribbon and form long, thin stems in straight stitch, and twisted straight stitch. To form the curved stems, make a loose twisted straight stitch, and bring the ribbon to the front of the work at the next stem. Keep a loose tension. Thread up with the green thread and use tiny stab stitches to couch the curved stem in place every 5 mm or so.

Note: *The thicker stems are (flat, untwisted) straight stitches.*

Now work the leaves in the 7-mm green ribbon and the usual straight stitch. For the folded leaves use folded straight stitch. Form the stitch with a fold first, then use the green thread and tiny stab stitches along the edge of the ribbon to secure the folded leaf in place. Make the back row first, stitching over the stems, and add the front leaves on top.

Form the flowers next. Change to the blue 4-mm ribbon and use one or two straight stitches to make the petals that are overlapped by others, then overlap them with two or three folded or twisted ribbon stitches to form the curved petals on the side and in front. Use the blue thread and tiny stab stitches along the edge of the curved stitches to secure the ribbon to the fabric. At the same time secure any looped stitches at the back, so the stitches don't pull out of shape as you work.

Hint: *When using thread to secure the ribbon stitches, always ensure the ribbon lies on the top of the work. Make the curved stitch and take the ribbon to the back. Use a gentle tension. Bring the needle to the front of the work all set for the next petal. This way the ribbon won't be tangled at the back of the work as you stitch with the needle and thread.*

Change to the green thread and use long detached chain/lazy daisy stitch to form any long, fine stems branching from the main stem. Use the same thread and straight /stab stitch at the tip of each petal to add texture and to stabilize the stitch.

To complete the bluebells, use the blue thread and a grab stitch to neaten the base of each bluebell. Catch all the petals at once and pull the stitch taut before inserting it to the back a short distance away.

PANEL ELEVEN

Pennywort

Cosmos

Pennywort begonia

Begonia hydrocotylifolia

Also known as pond lily begonia because of its appearance. Discovered in Mexico in 1841, the pennywort begonia is an evergreen semi-tuberous perennial that grows close to the ground and has small, rounded, heart-shaped leaves that are deep red underneath, with darker veins on top. It flowers in spring and early summer and thrives in warm, moist conditions with early morning or late afternoon sun. In temperate climates the plant may grow all year round. It is easily propagated, as it roots freely in sandy soil.

REQUIREMENTS
Mill Hill petite glass beads yellow no 62039 Mill Hill glass seed beads green no 02053

CHAMELEON THREADS
Pure silk: Black Berry no 8, Forest Shade no 33, Gold Nugget no 2 Perlé: Lemons no 45 Use 1 strand of thread unless otherwise specified
DI VAN NIEKERK'S RIBBONS
Silk 4-mm no 72
STITCHES
Stem stitch, straight/stab stitch, ribbon stitch, blanket stitch, back stitch
NEEDLES
Use the no 9 or no 10 crewel for one strand of thread, the no 10 for beading, the no 22 or no 24 chenille for perlé thread Use the no 20 or no 22 chenille for the 4-mm ribbon

Work the stems in fine whipped stem or back stitch with the black berry thread. For stem stitch, use the modern version where the stitches are not too much at an angle. Keep the needle and thread on the outside (widest part) of the curve each time to form soft, rounded curves. Keep the stitches small and pull the thread taut before making the next stitch. Whip the stem in the same thread.

Change to the green perlé thread and use a blanket stitch to form the leaves. Start at the stem and work along the edge, fanning the stitches out for a rounded tip. Insert the needle back at the centre vein each time.

Change to the Black Berry thread and add the purple veins on top in straight stitch. For an interesting texture, thread up with the darker green silk thread and add a few straight stitches between the light green stitches inserting the needle on the inside edge of the blanket stitch each time.

Outline the leaf in the same darker green silk and stem stitch to form the shadows.

Work the petals in the purple ribbon and ribbon stitch, from the centre outwards. Make tiny stab stitches at the tips of the ribbon petals in the golden thread to secure and add an attractive edge. Attach two beads in the centre of each flower with the same thread and the no 10 crewel needle.

The buds are made in the same purple ribbon and small ribbon stitches. Make two stitches overlapping each other to form a rounded bud. Change to the yellow thread and add a green bead at the base of the bud to form the calyx.

Cosmos bipinnatus

Common name: Common cosmos, Mexican cosmos

Native to Mexico and the South Western United States, Cosmos bipinnatus *is a much-loved, fast-growing annual with white, magenta, pink, lavender, lilac or purple daisy-like flowers that are 5-7,5 cm (2-3 in) in diameter. Perfectly formed, with long, willowy stems and lacy leaves, they make good cut flowers provided they are picked when just open. Cosmos need full sun for the flowers to open and as they like dry and infertile soils, they are easy to grow, requiring little attention, fertilisers or water. They flower in summer and early autumn and attract butterflies, bees and birds to the garden. The name* cosmos *comes from the Greek word* kosmos *meaning* harmony *or* beautiful thing.

Hint: *Use this technique for beautiful scrapbook pages, card-making and on trinket boxes. The cosmos is quick and easy to make and will add an exciting feature to your project! Instead of using stitches, glue the ribbon stems and petals in place with acid-free multi-purpose glue, adding the flower centres last.*

REQUIREMENTS
20 x 20 cm soft white polycotton or cotton 25 x 25 cm medium-weight iron-on interfacing 25 x 25 cm water-soluble fabric Sharp 2B or 3B pencil or blue pen with water-soluble ink Water-soluble multipurpose glue stick (similar to the ones used at school) 5 x 5 cm white felt
CHAMELEON THREADS
Pure silk: Cyclamen no 22, Goldrush no 37, Egg Yolk no 28, Seaweed no 107 Use 1 strand of thread unless otherwise specified
DI VAN NIEKERK'S RIBBONS
Silk 4-mm no 18, 25-mm no 108 and 7-mm no 30
STITCHES
Straight/stab stitch, French knot, satin stitch, ribbon stitch, back stitch, straight stitch – twisted, couching, fly stitch, pistil stitch.
NEEDLES
Use a no 9 or no 10 (fine) crewel for the thread Use the no 18 chenille for the 7-mm ribbon, no 20 or no 22 chenille for 4-mm ribbon

Form the thin stems above the thicker V-shaped base first. Thread up with the green silk ribbon and insert the needle from the back just above the thick base. Use a twisted straight stitch and insert the needle to the back on the outside of the yellow centre of the cosmos. The pink petals will be added on top later. Keep a loose tension and couch in place every 5 to 10 mm (¼ to ½ in) with the Seaweed thread. Do the

same for the other stems and leaves, twirling the ribbon quite tight for the thinner stems and leaves. The green calyx petals underneath the pink petals are made in ribbon stitch. Start at the centre and work outwards. Stitch over the cosmos petals, as these will be added on top later.

Use the same green ribbon and form the main V-shaped stem in fly stitch. Add the straight stem beneath the V in one ribbon stitch. Use the green thread and tiny stab stitches at the top and base of this ribbon stitch to secure and shape. Make another ribbon stitch on top of this one and secure as before with the green thread. Make another fly stitch on top of the previous V-shaped stitch to add a heavier

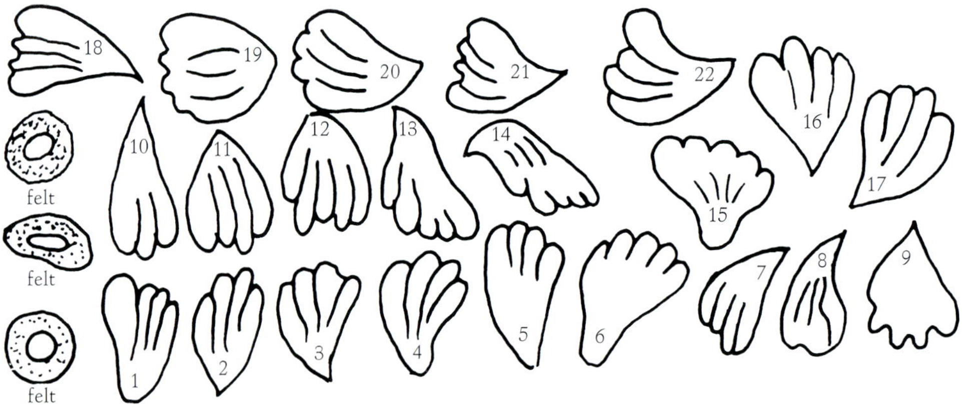

texture. Add a third fly stitch on top if necessary. Use the green thread to anchor and shape any sagging ribbon and to neaten the stem.

Note: *The cosmos petals are made individually on interfacing that is ironed onto pure silk ribbon, cut out and then applied to the design – a form of free-standing appliqué. The shapes are easy to make, even for inexperienced needle crafters, and the technique saves a huge amount of time and effort normally spent on filling shapes with embroidery stitches. The free standing appliqué shapes add an interesting texture and combine well with ribbon embroidery and stumpwork. (See camellia on page 43 for more hints.)*

Trace the cosmos petals (22) and centres (3) above with all the detail and the numbers on the smooth, non-fusible side (not the shiny or rough side) side of the interfacing.

Use a soft, sharp 2B or 3B pencil and trace each shape as neatly as possible leaving a space of 5 mm or so between the shapes. Draw the veins of the petals and number each petal in the position shown above. This is so the number won't show through the ribbon petal once completed as these sections will be covered by the centre of the flower later.

Cut out the interfacing shapes a few millimetres from the edge. Don't cut on the pencil line. To prevent fraying, you will only cut along the pencil line once the interfacing has been ironed onto the ribbon or felt. Place these shapes in a small bowl as you cut them out, as they do tend to get lost rather easily. (Don't sneeze!)

Place the 25 mm ribbon (lightest side up) on the ironing board and set the iron on a medium setting with the steam off. (A dry iron is essential.) Place an interfacing petal pencil side up (shiny or rough side down) on top of the pink silk ribbon. Press each interfacing petal onto the ribbon so the heat bonds it well. Iron the three round centres onto the white felt block. Check that each shape is attached to the ribbon and felt and that the interfacing shape does not lift at the edges.

Cut out all the shapes along the pencil lines as neatly as possible with small, sharp embroidery scissors. Hold a petal against a sunny window or light box and draw in the straight lines (the veins) on the pink side (right side) of the petal, using a soft pencil. Don't repeat the number on the right side. Do this for all the petals.

Insert the water-soluble fabric in a 20 cm (8 in) hoop. Place the ribbon shapes, ribbon-side up on the water-soluble layer and the felt shapes felt-side up. Leave a space of 1 cm between the shapes. Use the glue stick to lightly glue the shapes to the water-soluble fabric.

Thread up with the pink thread and work the veins on the pink petals in back stitch. Start at the sharp tip and work upwards. Work downwards again, stitch over one or two back stitches to reach the bottom tip before starting the next vein. End by neatly working the thread into the stitches at the back. Do the same for all the petals.

Thread up with Egg Yolk yellow thread and work the inner circles of the cosmos centres in satin stitch. Work another row of satin stitch on top in the opposite direction. Change to the golden yellow thread and make French knots (one wrap) to form the stamens above and on the side of the centres. Make 2 or 3 rows in a circular shape. Add more stamens in the front with pistil stitch if you prefer, working from the outside upwards.

Cut out the pink and felt shapes leaving a 5 mm edge of water soluble fabric. Place shapes in a bowl of water for about one minute.

Hint: *It is not necessary to dissolve the water-soluble fabric completely. Once dry, the sticky residue won't be noticeable but it will hold the petals firm for a raised texture once they are attached to the design.*

Remove shapes and allow place on a towel or dishcloth to dry, but before they are completely dry, bend the tips of petals 5, 6, 9, 14 and 15 so the lighter, interfacing side is facing upwards.

Once the folded petals are attached, they add a very realistic touch.

Use the numbered diagram on page 97 to place the petals. Using the number on the back of the petal shapes, place and attach one petal at a time with the pink thread using tiny stab stitches along the base of each petal. Overlap the petals where necessary and in the centre of the flowers. Allow the scalloped outer edge of the petals to stand free. Attach in the following sequence: petal 1 first, followed by petals 3, 2, 4, 5, 6, 8, and 7. Attach petal 9 next, followed by 10, 11, 12, 13, 14 and no 15. The third flower is assembled by placing petal 17 first, followed by no 16, 18, 20, 19, 21, and finally no 22.

Attach the yellow centres on top, using the golden yellow thread and small stab stitches, adding more French knots along the sides to hide the white edges.

PANEL TWELVE

English daisy

Freesia

Honeybee

English daisy

Bellis perennis

The scientific name bellis *is from the Latin word meaning* beautiful, *an apt description of this charming little European wild flower, a low-growing perennial with small daisy-like flowers on slender stems. Flowers appear in spring and are white (often with pink or red tips) or shades of pink. The flower heads are 2 to 3cm in diameter with yellow centres. They sometimes grow in fields and lawn.* Bellis perennis *makes a good ground cover and is suitable for rock gardens or as an edging plant. It prefers moist, fertile soil in full sun to light shade.*

Hint: *Use this technique to make beautiful flowers for scrapbook pages, card-making and for embellishing quilts, jerseys or to stitch onto a dress panel or pocket. Embroider on a separate piece of fabric and attach to your page with acid-free glue. Alternatively use the method described for Oxalis (see page 20) and assemble the daisies afterwards.*

CHAMELEON THREADS
Pure silk: Green Olives no 97, Protea no 4, Egg Yolk 28 Use 1 strand of thread unless otherwise specified
DI VAN NIEKERK'S RIBBONS
Silk: 2-mm no 104
STITCHES
Stem stitch – whipped, straight/stab stitch, French knot, ribbon stitch, detached chain/lazy daisy, fly stitch, grab stitch
NEEDLES
Use the no 9 or no 10 (fine) crewel for one strand of thread Use the no 22 or no 24 chenille for the 2-mm ribbon

Using the green thread and whipped stem stitch, work the stems first. Add the leaves in same thread and detached chain/lazy daisy.

Form the white petals in ribbon stitch with the thin white ribbon. Note how the ribbon changes subtly from white to light grey. This adds the shadows that create a life-like flower. Use the same ribbon and stitch for the buds.

Change to the pink thread and use a fly stitch or detached chain/lazy daisy along the tip of each daisy petal and bud. Make the stitch on top of the white ribbon and not on the edge.

Change to the green thread and add the green calyx at the base of each bud in grab stitch or fly stitch. Add a few straight stitches in-between for more colour.

Complete the yellow centres in the yellow thread and tiny French knots (1 or 2 wraps around the needle) Stitching on the edge of the white ribbon stitches to secure the petals.

Freesias

Family: Iridaceae

Native to South Africa, freesias are now widely grown the world over, with more than 300 hybrids in a wide range of brilliant colours. The corm-forming plants flower in spring and the tubular purple, violet, lavender, mauve, red, yellow, pink and white flowers are prized for their intense sweet perfume and long vase life. Stems are upright, slender, strong and arched, 20 to 45 cm high with long, pointed leaves. Six or more single or double flower-heads grow along one side of the stem. The plants are dormant in summer and are best treated as annuals.

Hint: *Freesias are ideal flowers to embroider on jerseys for they are easy to make and blend well with the texture of the wool. Curtain tie-backs will look perfect with a row of freesias as they fill up quickly and are large enough for the curved shape of the tie-back. The gorgeous colours of the freesias can only enhance your masterpiece! Instead of adding the cake decorating stamens that are suggested in the instructions, use lavender or white thread and pistil stitch instead.*

REQUIREMENTS
Stamens from cake decorating stores – white and lavender
CHAMELEON THREADS
Pure silk: Egg Yolk no 28, Knysna Forest no 3 Cyclamen no 22, Wisteria no 95 and Cobalt no 19 Use 1 strand of thread unless otherwise specified
DI VAN NIEKERK'S RIBBONS
Silk: 2-mm no 36, no 17 (or 1 m sage green wool for stems); 4-mm no 32, no 51, no 54; 13-mm no 55, no 123, no 112
STITCHES
Couching, straight/stab stitch, straight stitch – twisted, straight stitch – padded, ribbon stitch, blanket stitch, fly stitch, and grab stitch
NEEDLES
Use the fine no 9 or no 10 crewel for the threads Use a no 16 or no 18 (thick) chenille for the 13-mm ribbon, no 20 or no 22 for the wool or 4-mm ribbon, no 22 or no 24 (fine) for the 2-mm ribbon

Start with the slender dark green leaves. Thread up with the thin green ribbon and use straight stitch for the flatter leaves and twisted straight stitch for the finer leaves. Use 1 strand of the green thread and tiny stab stitches to secure in place every centimetre or so.

Make the freesia stems. Thread up with the green wool or no 17 silk ribbon and couch in place with the green thread. Stitch over the freesia flowers as these will be made on top later.

Hint: *Refer to the numbered Freesia diagram overleaf for the sequence of stitches and flowers. Make the small buds first.*

Thread up with the 13-mm ribbon no 112 and form buds 12, 11 and 10 in ribbon stitch. Use the same stitch for buds 17, 16, 15 and 14, ending the tail of ribbon at the back with thread and small stab stitches. Change to the yellow 13-mm ribbon and make a ribbon or straight stitch on top of each of these buds, overlapping the pink to add more colour. Embroider bud 4 with a yellow ribbon stitch, and change to the lavender ribbon to add two more straight stitches on top of the yellow stitch. Form bud 6 with the lavender ribbon and padded straight stitch. Use three or four straight stitches overlapping each other for a fat, rounded bud. Complete the buds with the green 4-mm ribbon and fly stitch or grab stitch to form the green calyx. Buds 14 and 15 are finished in the same green ribbon, but use a long fly stitch so the buds are surrounded with green petals.

Thread up with the 13-mm ribbon no 112 and work the flowers in ribbon stitch, starting with freesias 8 and 9 in pink and yellow. Refer to the photograph for colour guidelines. Keep the tension loose for soft, rounded petals.

Use the same pink ribbon and ribbon stitch for the lower four petals of for freesia 7. Change to the lilac ribbon no 123 and form the two lilac petals on top of the pink ones. Form the lilac petals on freesia 3 using the same ribbon and stitch, then freesia 1, 5 and 2. Stitch over the petals of freesia 1.

Change to the no 55 ribbon and complete the yellow no 13 freesia and the top petals of no 3 in ribbon stitch. Add the bottom yellow stitch on freesia 5. Change to the green 4-mm ribbon and form the calyx of no 3, 5, 9 and 13. Use a fly, grab or straight stitch as for the buds.

Add an interesting edge to some of the petals with the cyclamen, wisteria, cobalt and egg yolk thread. Use a blanket stitch working from the base to the tip and down again. Keep the tension loose to avoid distorting the ribbon petals. Thread up with the orange or yellow ribbon (the orange ribbon for the yellow petals and the yellow ribbon for the lavender and pink petals) and use a straight stitch to form the bands of colour on the open freesias. A single straight stitch is made on top of each petal to form the centre.

Use the same stitch and yellow thread in-between to add more colour if you like.

Insert the stamens. Use the no 16 chenille needle (or the sharp tip of the small embroidery scissors) to make a hole in the centre of the freesia. Take care not to pull the petals out of shape. If this does happen, simply make another stitch on top later. Insert the folded stamen in the hole. Alternatively, fold the stamen in half and thread the folded section through the eye of the needle. Take the needle to the back, working with a gentle tension. Hold on to the stamen tips on the right side so they are not pulled through by mistake. Add another folded stamen in the same way as before.

Gently pull the stamens back to the front until you are happy with the length. Bend the stamens at the back and secure with stab stitch. Cut off the excess at the back. Turn the hoop so the right side is showing and use the yellow thread and tiny stab stitches to secure the stamens to the centre of each flower.

Honeybee

Apis mellifera

Honeybee is the common name for a species of insect from the Apidae family. Honeybees are social insects forming colonies where they build nests from the wax they secrete. Pollen and nectar are collected from flowers and stored as honey. Honeybees are essential in nature and for agriculture as they pollinate wild plants and crops. Bees are ideal insects for stumpwork, as their translucent wings are easy to make and are a charming feature in any project.

REQUIREMENTS
20 x 20 cm each white organza and water-soluble fabric Sharp HB pencil #30 wire from cake decorating shops Fray Stop or anti-fray agent

CHAMELEON THREADS
Pure silk: Scottish Heather no 68, Sunburst no 4, Charcoal no 15 Use 1 strand of thread unless otherwise specified
METALLIC THREADS
Kreinik blending filament no 32 Pearl
STITCHES
Couching, straight/stab stitch, satin stitch, pistil stitch, blanket/buttonhole stitch, open buttonhole stitch, French knot, pistil stitch
NEEDLES
Use the no 9 crewel for the metallic thread and a no 9 or no 10 crewel for the silk threads

Trace the 2 wings in the centre of the organza, place organza, pencil side up, on top of the water-soluble fabric, insert both layers in a 15 cm (6 in) hoop, gently pull both layers taut and tighten the hoop. Prepare the #30 wire as described on page 21. Insert 2 or 3 cm of the wire to the back of the work on the sharp inside tip of the wing and secure to the back with masking tape. Couch the wire in place every 3 mm or so with the light grey thread and insert the wire to the back again. Cut off the excess wire, leaving a 2 to 3 cm tail and tape in place as before. Cover the wire in buttonhole stitch (see buttonhole stitch over wire on page 153). Form the veins on the wings in the pearl metallic thread and open buttonhole stitch or fly stitch. Keep a loose tension for a frilly finish. Repeat with the other wing and set aside to be cut out later.

Work on the main design. Thread up with the charcoal thread and form the black stripes on the bee's body in tiny satin stitches (vertical-facing head to tail) or French knots (one wrap) made close together. Form the antennae in pistil stitch and the legs in straight stitch. Change to the yellow thread and complete the yellow stripes as you did the black stripes.

Remove the tape and cut out the wings taking care not to cut the stitches. Dip the wings in a cup of tepid water for thirty seconds or so to dissolve the water-soluble fabric. Allow to dry.

Make two small holes on the main design alongside the bee's body with the sharp point of small embroidery scissors or use a size 16 or 18 chenille needle. Place the two wings by inserting the wire ends into the holes. Bend the wire backwards on the wrong side of the work so it lies beneath the wing section and attach in place with small stab stitches.

Use nail clippers or old scissors to trim the excess wire. Bend the wings into a pleasing shape.

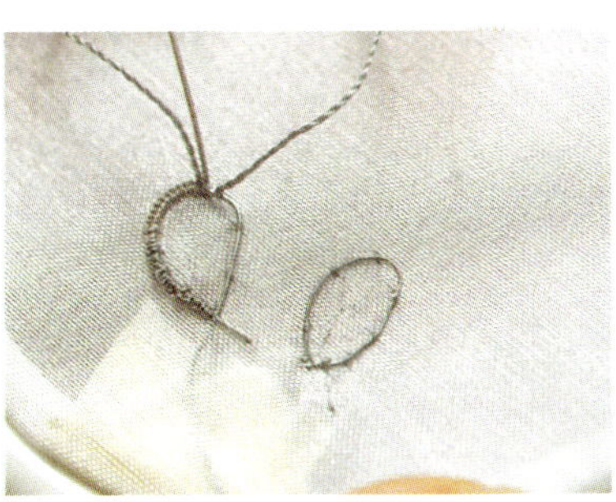

PANEL THIRTEEN

Leucadendrons

Ants

Leucadendron levisanus

Common name: Cape Flats conebush, spatula-leaf protea, sandknoppiesbos

This beautiful, endangered plant is endemic to South Africa and forms part of the fynbos flora. It is a tall, upright flowering shrub about 2 metres high and grows in damp, sandy, acid soil on the Cape Peninsula, where urban development has taken its toll on the plant's distribution. Leucadendrons have separate male and female plants. The male flowerhead of L. levisanus *depicted here has bright yellow flowers, making for a magnificent display in spring and early summer.*

Hint: *This eye-catching flower is ideal for embellishing quilts or jerseys or a dress panel or pocket. The long stems and large leaves fill a design quite quickly and the flowerheads will add a lovely texture too.*

CHAMELEON THREADS
Pure silk: Velvet Brown no 111, Egg Yolk no 28 Use 1 strand of thread unless otherwise specified
DI VAN NIEKERK'S RIBBONS
Silk: 4-mm no 109, 2-mm no 104 Organza: 7-mm no 16
STITCHES
Straight/stab stitch, French knot, detached chain/lazy daisy, ribbon stitch and turkey stitch.
NEEDLES
Use the no 9 or no 10 (fine) crewel for one strand and the no 8 or no 9 for two strands of thread Use the no 18 chenille for the 7-mm ribbon, the no 20 or no 22 chenille for the 4-mm ribbon and the no 22 or no 24 for the 2-mm ribbon

Work the flower stems using one or two strands of the brown thread and chain stitch. Start at the base and work upwards, stitching over the large flower which will be added on top later. Do the same for all the stems.

Use the same thread to add a few straight stitches or lazy daisy stitches to form the knobbly texture on the lower stems.

Work the leaves in the green organza ribbon and ribbon stitch. Change to the brown thread and add a few stab stitches at the tips and base to stabilize the leaves and to add a life-like texture.

Form the flowerheads. Thread up with the white and grey ribbon (no 104) and use French knots (one or two wraps) close together to form the inner circle of the flowers. Change to the cream silk ribbon and work the row of petals behind the French knots in stab stitch, then the front petals.

Thread up with two strands of the yellow thread and work a row of turkey stitch at the base of the petals just above the leaves to form the fluffy yellow texture. Work another row above this one, just beneath the cream petals and stagger the stitches so the rows are not too bulky. Make loops about 8 to 10 mm long and cut and trim the loops every now and then to ensure the end result is not too bulky. Fluff the stitches gently with the sharp point of the embroidery scissors or chenille needle.

Leucadendron discolor

Common name: Piketberg conebush

Another indigenous South African flower belonging to the Proteaceae *family and endemic to the Piketberg region.* Discolor *means* two colours*, probably referring to the male flower heads that are very colourful in spring with orange-red flowers and broad yellow oval bracts. Popular as a cut-flower* Leucadendron discolor *is a bushy, upright, evergreen shrub, growing up to 2 m tall and flowering in September and October. It likes sandy soil and stores its seed in cones. After a fire the seeds are released to grow again. Without fires this species will become extinct. It is also threatened by alien invaders such as pines.*

Note: *The stuffed, raised cone of the flower is too thick for a chenille needle to pierce, making it difficult to use the normal ribbon stitch bracts. For this reason the two yellow/rust bracts in front of the cone are made separately. They are traced onto interfacing, cut out and ironed onto organza ribbon. The interfacing is used to prevent fraying of the organza ribbon and to stabilize the ribbon bracts. The bracts are then cut out and attached to the design – a form of free-standing appliqué.*

REQUIREMENTS
20 x 20 cm soft white polycotton or cotton 10 x 10 cm medium-weight iron-on interfacing 20 x 20 cm water-soluble fabric Sharp 2B or 3B pencil or blue pen with water-soluble ink Water-soluble multipurpose glue stick (similar to the ones used at school) Small piece of toy filling or wadding to fill the shape
CHAMELEON THREADS
Pure silk: Velvet Brown no 111, Tropical Green no 3 Stranded cotton: Baked Earth no 7 Use 1 strand of thread unless otherwise specified
DI VAN NIEKERK'S RIBBONS
Silk 2-mm no 51 and 57 Organza 25-mm no 53
STITCHES
Stem stitch, straight/stab stitch, French knot, satin stitch, ribbon stitch, blanket stitch, back stitch
NEEDLES
Use a no 9 or no 10 (fine) crewel for one strand of thread and a no 8 or no 9 for two strands Use the no 16 chenille for the 25-mm ribbon and a no 22 or no 24 chenille for 2-mm ribbon

Form the stem first in the velvet brown thread with rows of stem stitch made close together, working from the base towards the flower. Use the same thread and satin stitch in the opposite direction to add more texture.

Form the four large yellow/rust bracts at the back of the orange cone in ribbon stitch. Use the 25-mm organza ribbon and thread up the no 16 chenille needle (fold ribbon in half and use a no 18 if you don't have a size 16 needle). Work on top of the cone shape on the design as the cone is made separately and attached later. Leave a tail at the back. Use the brown thread to secure the tail to the back of the work and cut off the excess before making the ribbon stitch. Gently pull the ribbon through to the back so a soft, rounded bract is formed.

Thread up with a strand of the Baked Earth brown thread and work blanket stitch around the edges of the ribbon bracts. Use a gentle tension so the ribbon is not pulled out of shape. Start at the cone and work anti-clockwise (clockwise if you are left-handed) around the leaf ending at the base next to the cone again. Use the same thread to anchor the tip of the bract to the background just along the inside of the tip in straight/stab stitch.

Trace the cone shape of the flower above in the centre of the white fabric block. Use a sharp HB or 2B pencil and draw in the detail of the petals – these will be the direction lines to guide you as you embroider the shape. Trace the oval outline too, as this will be the cutting line later. Insert in a 15 cm (6 in) hoop.

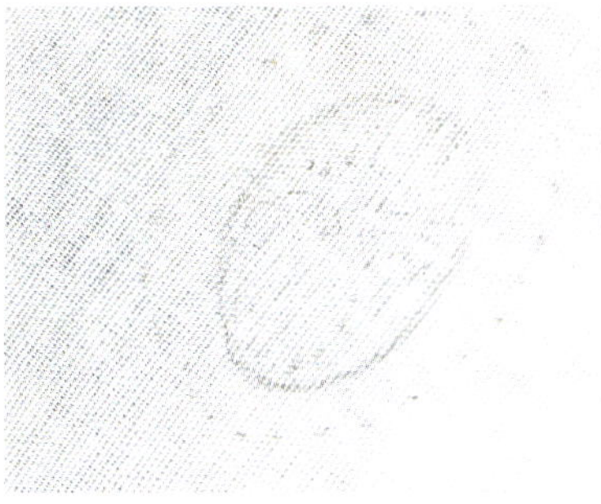

Thread up with two strands of the Baked Earth thread and work straight/stab stitches close together to form the brown oval. Add a few French knots (one wrap) and stab stitches between the petals to create the brown shadows. Change to the darker orange ribbon and starting at the top, work down and outwards to form the orange petals above the brown centre in stab stitch. Work along the sides of the brown centre in the same stitch and allow the petals to face outwards towards the left and right of the brown centre.

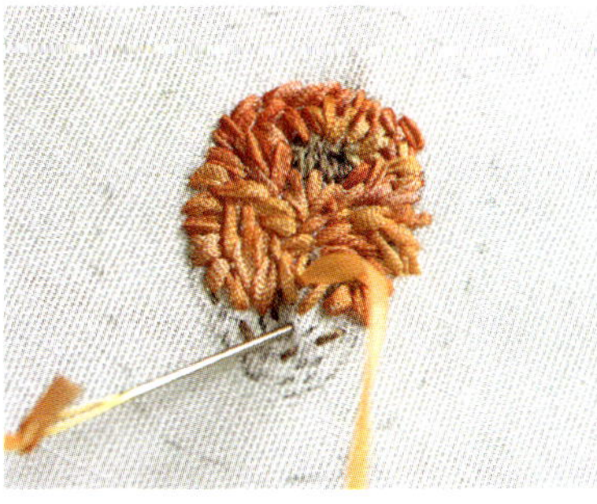

Work beneath the oval; follow the direction lines drawn on the shape. Change to the lighter orange ribbon and complete the cone as before working downwards towards the base. Change to two strands of the green thread and add a few lime green stab stitches in-between the orange petals. Use the brown thread to add more shadows in stab stitch inbetween the orange petals if necessary.

Cut out the cone along the outside line. Cut small slits in the seam every centimetre or so.

Fold the seams to the back of the shape and place the cone on the design, partly covering the four embroidered bracts. Use the orange ribbon and stab stitch to secure in place along the edge of the cone. Allow the stab stitches to face the same way as the petals so they blend in well.

Leave a small gap to fill the shape, so a rounded cone is formed. Insert toy filling or shredded wadding inside the shape until it is nice and fat. Close the gap with the same ribbon. Use the same stitch and ribbon to cover any white seams that are showing at the tip stitching through all the layers, keeping a gentle tension to avoid distorting the shape.

Trace the two bract shapes on page 108 on the smooth non-fusible side (not the shiny or rough side) of the interfacing. Use a soft, sharp 2B or 3B pencil or blue pen with water-soluble ink, and trace the shapes as neatly as possible leaving a space of a centimetre or so between the shapes.

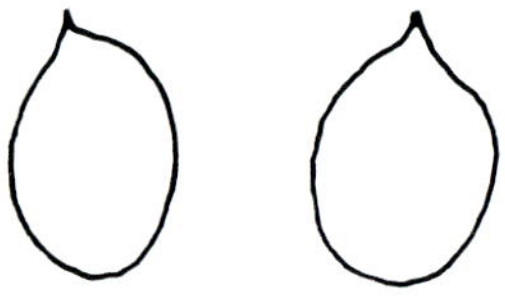

Cut out the interfacing shapes a few millimetres from the edge. Don't cut on the pencil line. To prevent fraying, you will only cut along the pencil line once the interfacing has been ironed onto the ribbon. Place the organza ribbon on the ironing board with the interfacing shapes on top, shiny or rough side down. Use an iron on a medium setting with the steam off (a dry iron is essential) to press each shape onto the ribbon so the heat bonds it well. Be careful not to scorch the ribbon. Check that the shapes are attached to the ribbon and that the shapes do not lift at the edges.

Cut out each shape along the pencil line as neatly as possible with small, sharp embroidery scissors. Insert the water-soluble fabric in a 15 cm (6 in) hoop. Place the two shapes, ribbon side up on the water-soluble layer. Leave a 1 cm space between the shapes and lightly glue to the water-soluble fabric with the glue stick. If too much glue is used, it dissolves the water-soluble fabric. Simply lift the shape and place elsewhere on the fabric. Thread up with the brown baked earth thread and work blanket stitch around the edge of the shapes. Start at the rounded base with a knot and work anti-clockwise (clockwise if you are left-handed) around the shape. End off with a few back stitches on the base.

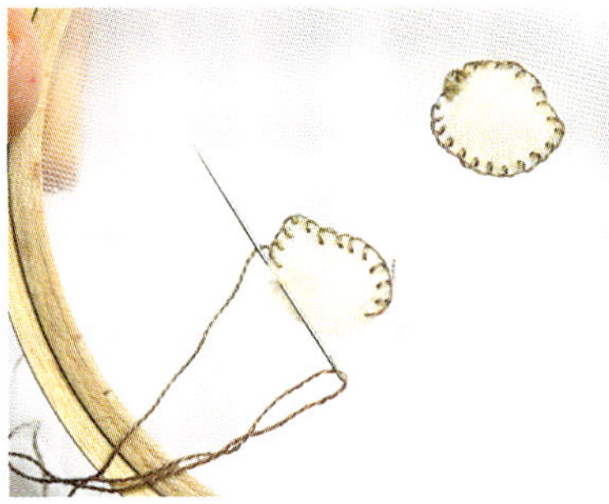

Cut out the shapes leaving a half cm edge of water soluble fabric.

Place shapes in a bowl of water for four or five minute. Remove and allow the shapes to dry on a towel or dishcloth.

Use the same brown thread and tiny stab stitches along the base of the bracts to attach over the rounded cone, stitching beneath the cone so bracts seem to emerge from under the cone as shown.

Stitch along the outer edges of the bracts to anchor them to the design, allowing the inside edges on the cone to be free.

Ants

Family: Formicidae

There are roughly 8 000 different species of ant worldwide. The earliest ant-like fossils date back over a hundred million years! Ants are social insects and live in structured nests or colonies, some with more than a million ants. They differ in length from a large 2,5 centimetres to a tiny 2 mm and are black, red, brown or yellow in colour. Ants are elongated with a large head and a characteristic thin waist. Ants are essential in the conservation of some members of the protea family, as they carry the seeds to their underground nests where the seed remains safe until conditions are right for them to germinate.

Hint: *Use the water-soluble technique to make separate little ant bodies for scrapbook pages or for card making. Instead of embroidering the ants directly on the design as shown here, insert water-soluble fabric in a 15 cm (6 in) hoop. Trace and embroider the body and cut out the shapes leaving a 5-mm edge. Place the shapes in a bowl of water for a few minutes to dissolve the film. Attach to your page with acid-free glue and draw in the legs and feeler with a black fine-liner. Embroider directly on the fabric to embellish quilts, jerseys or onto a dress panel or pocket.*

CHAMELEON THREADS
Pure silk: Charcoal no 15, Gold Nugget no 2 Use one strand of thread throughout
STITCHES
Couching, stem stitch, straight/stab stitch, French knot, split stitch, back stitch, seeding, single knotted stitch.
NEEDLES
Use the no 9 or no 10 (fine) crewel

Thread up with the charcoal thread and outline the head in fine stem-, split- or back stitch. Fill with French knots (one wrap). Use the same thread and two or three tiny stab stitches to form the eye. Pull the stitches taut, so the stitches form a dent on the French knots.

The feeler is worked in a single knotted stitch, (one Turkey stitch.) Cut and trim the loop.

Work the trunk and the metasoma like the head, outlining the three rounded shapes first then filling with French knots. Be sure to have a narrow waist before the large part of the abdomen, as this is the distinctive feature of the ant.

Add the legs last in the same thread and straight stitch. To form the bent legs, use a straight stitch that is couched in place. To couch a straight stitch, make a straight stitch as normal but use a loose tension. Take the needle to the back. Insert the needle and thread to the front again exactly where you would like the fold to be. Use the needle to pull the straight stitch into a bent line before inserting the needle to the back into the same hole again.

Complete the panel by adding the sand beneath the flowers. Use the golden thread and seeding stitch to form the fine grains of the sand.

PANEL FOURTEEN

Fish

Dierama

Bulrushes

Frog & waterlily

A fish in the water

Species non-specificus

Did you know that there are more species of fish than mammals, reptiles and birds put together? The most plentiful of all vertebrate (backboned) animals, there are more than 20 000 different fish species, including a living fossil, the coelacanth. Some species of fish are thought to live for over 100 years. The smallest fish is the goby from the Philippine Islands at less than 10 mm in length and the largest is the whale shark reaching lengths of 15 to 18 metres. Around one third of the fish caught today is used to feed pets and livestock and more than 2 billion people depend on fish as a source of protein.

REQUIREMENTS
15 x 8 cm white organza Temporary fabric spray adhesive (Sulky KK 2000) optional Fray Stop or anti-fray agent
CHAMELEON THREADS
Pure silk: Peacock no 103, Tropical green no 3, Arctic Blue no 5 or Cobalt no 19 Use one strand of thread throughout.
RAJMAHAL ART SILK
Gothic Grey no 226
STITCHES
Stem or split stitch, French knot, running stitch, straight/ stab stitch, turkey stitch
NEEDLES
Use a no 9 or 10 crewel needle

Note: *The fish and the dark ripples in the water are embroidered on the design first and then a layer of white organza fabric is placed on top to depict water.*

Thread up with the grey thread and outline the fish in stem or split stitch Embroider the scales in tiny straight/ stab stitch, the tail in longer straight/ stab stitch and make a small French knot (two wraps) for the eye. Embroider the dark ripples in the water in the grey thread using horizontal straight/ stab stitch.

Press the organza with a cool iron to remove any creases and lay the fabric on top of the water and the fish. Align the edge of the organza fabric with the edge of the water (at the base of the long grass) covering the water lily and the frog (these will be attached on top later). Ensure that the outer line of the blue border is covered too and leave a small seam allowance that will be cut away later.

Hint: *Lightly spray the back of the organza fabric with a temporary fabric spray adhesive like Sulky KK 2000 and press down on top of the panel. This prevents the organza from moving. If you do not have any spray adhesive, pin the organza fabric to the design on the outer border line and remove the pins as you stitch.*

Thread up with the light blue thread and use small running stitches along the outer border lines (these stitches will be covered later with dark blue thread once the border is completed – see page 146). Use the same thread and stitch along the edge of the water beneath the long grass.

Hint: *Stitch over the frog and the lily, as these will be added on top later. Use the same blue thread and small horizontal stab stitches to form the lighter blue ripples on the water. Work on top of the organza fabric. This stabilizes the organza and adds an interesting texture.*

Use small sharp scissors and carefully cut along the outer edge of the stitched organza.

Use an anti-fray agent that dries clear (test first) along the edge of the organza although do remember that the line on the border will be covered later with dark blue thread.

Thread up with 2 strands of the green thread and use long turkey stitches to form the long green grass along the water's edge. Pull the loops up before cutting them. This way the stitches are facing upwards to form the long, upright grass. Use the Peacock blue thread and add two or three straight stitches at the water's edge for shadows.

Dierama pendulum

Common names: angel's fishing rods, African hairbell, fairybells, fairy wands, wedding bells and grasklokkies

Dierama *is a Greek word meaning* funnel, *describing the shape of the flowers. There are over 40 species of* Dierama, *all indigenous to Africa – from the mountains of East Africa to the Eastern Cape – with* D. pendulum *among the most beautiful and most popular. Now widely grown in the UK and New Zealand,* Dierama *have graceful bell-shaped flowers in the palest pinks to magenta, lavender and violet. Growing in grass-like clusters on graceful wand-like stems above sword-shaped leaves, the flowers appear in late spring or early summer. Dierama can grow up to 2 m tall.*

Hint: *Embroider these graceful flowers on jerseys, cushions, linen and guest towels. For paper crafts like scrapbooking or card-making, use a gentle tension to embroider on strong hand-made paper (made easier by pre-punching holes).*

CHAMELEON THREADS
Pure silk: Rose no 64 Stranded cotton: Baked Earth no 7 Use 1 strand of thread unless otherwise specified
DI VAN NIEKERK'S RIBBONS
Silk 4-mm no 84 , 2-mm no 21
STITCHES
Straight/stab stitch, blanket stitch, French knot, detached chain/lazy daisy, stem stitch, back stitch, ribbon stitch, detached chain/lazy daisy, blanket stitch, grab stitch
NEEDLES
Use the no 9 or no 10 crewel for threads Use the no 20 or 22 chenille for the 4-mm ribbon and the no 22 or 24 chenille for the 2-mm ribbon

Start with the stems. Thread up with the brown thread and work the thin brown stem in stem stitch. Work another row of stem alongside the previous row at the base of the stem for a heavier texture. Use the same thread and back stitch to form the fine stems branching off the main stem.

Change to the brown ribbon and form the brown bracts beneath the pink petals in straight or back stitch.

Hint: *To turn a straight stitch into a curve, make the straight stitch as usual. Use the same ribbon and insert the needle from the back a short distance away from the straight stitch, close to where curve starts. Stitch over the straight stitch and insert the needle back into the same hole again. This way a straight stitch is transformed into a curve.*

Thread up with the pink ribbon and use one or two straight stitches to make the petals that are overlapped by other petals. Then overlap these with two or three ribbon stitches, some folded, some twisted to form the curved petals on either side and on top. Use the pink thread and tiny stab stitches or a detached chain/lazy daisy along the tips of the petals to secure the ribbon to the fabric.

Use the same thread and blanket stitch along the edge of one or two petals (optional) to add an interesting texture. At the same time secure any looped stitches at the back so the stitches don't pull out of shape as you work.

Finally, use the pink ribbon and a grab stitch to neaten the base of each flower. Grab all the petals at once and pull the stitch taut before inserting it to the back of the work again.

Bulrushes

Typha latifolia

Typha *species are found in marshy areas all over the world.* Typha latifolia, *a USA native also known as cat tail, is a water-loving plant found in swamps and wetlands. It has dark brown cigar-shaped flowers that bloom in spring and summer, and is a most useful plant. Birds, frogs, fish, insects and small mammals live in the dense bulrush marshes that provide nesting and cover. Fluff from the seed heads are used for stuffing pillows, and nappy liners. Its leaves are used to weave baskets, mats and chairs; it is also used to make rayon fibre, and its pulp is used in paper-making. Many parts are edible, also has medicinal properties.*

Hint: *Use this striking cat-tail design to embellish quilts, jerseys, cushions, linen, guest towels and clothing. To use this image for paper crafts like scrapbooking or card-making, follow the steps below, and embroider it on a background of sheer organza fabric, a fine wire mesh or 28 count evenweave fabric. Stretch and mount the fabric or mesh and glue onto your card or page with acid-free glue.*

CHAMELEON THREADS
Pure silk: Black Berry no 8, Granite no 105 Stranded cotton: Baked Earth no 7 Use 1 strand of thread unless otherwise specified
DI VAN NIEKERK'S RIBBONS
Silk: 2-mm no 118 and no 21
STITCHES
Straight/stab stitch, fly stitch and turkey stitch
NEEDLES
Use the no 9 or no 10 crewel for one strand of thread, and the no 22 or no 24 chenille for the 2-mm ribbon

Thread up with the green ribbon and make long straight stitches to form the stems. Twist some straight stitches to form a thinner stem. Keep a taut tension so the stems are not too loose. Work from the blue petals of the water lily upwards and insert the needle in the brown section of the bulrush.

Change to the Granite thread and work the cigar shaped flowers in turkey stitch. Start at the base and work upwards. Every now and then, cut the loops, trim and fluff them to ensure the texture is not too dense.

Hint: *Work 1 or 2 mm inside the shape as turkey stitch tends to enlarge a shape very quickly.*

Change to the brown ribbon and form the tufts above the brown flower in fly stitch. Work from the flower upwards ending in a straight stitch at the tip. Change to the brown thread and make a few stab stitches between the fly stitches to form the shadows. Work from the centre towards the outer edge.

Hint: *Remember to tighten the layers in the hoop every now and then, so the background does not pucker. Pull all the layers gently at each corner and tighten the hoop.*

Frog

Class: Amphibia, Order: Anura (frogs and toads)

Living both on land and in the water, frogs are amphibians, from the Greek words amphi *meaning* both *and* bios, *meaning* life. *There are about 4 000 known species of frogs and toads. They flourish in a temperate, damp and humid environment, but some also survive in deserts, such as the water-holding frog from southern Australia that buries itself in the hot dry ground, becoming inactive to conserve energy. It cocoons itself in a layer of shed skin which hardens and retains moisture, helping it survive. Found all over the world except in Iceland and the Antarctic, frogs are carnivorous, capturing small insects on their sticky tongues. The golden dart frog is the most poisonous frog on earth. The largest frog is the Goliath frog from West Africa, about 30 cm in length and the smallest a frog from Cuba at less than 9 mm long.*

REQUIREMENTS
Mill Hill petite glass beads no 42014 black Cloth print of frog on leaf and waterlily leaf 20 x 20 cm medium weight iron-on interfacing 20 x 20 cm block of water-soluble fabric Water-soluble multipurpose glue stick (similar to the ones used at school)
CHAMELEON THREADS
Stranded cotton: Baked Earth no 7, Moss no 54 Use 1 strand of thread unless otherwise specified
RAJMAHAL ART SILK
Rajmahal Art Silk Gothic Grey no 226
STITCHES
Straight/stab stitch, stem stitch or blanket/buttonhole stitch, French knot, back or split stitch
NEEDLES
Use the no 9 or no 10 crewel needle for one strand of thread

Hint: *Use this technique for beautiful scrapbook pages, for card-making and to decorate trinket boxes. Prepare the frog on its leaf and glue in place with acid-free glue, adding a waterlily (see page 117) alongside. For quilts, cushions, bags and jerseys, attach the shape to the background fabric with buttonhole/blanket stitch in a matching thread along the edge of the shape.*

Note: *For appliqué perse, the technique used for the frog, you need a colour print on cloth. Pre-printed full-colour panels with the different embroidery shapes, including the frog and the waterlily leaf, are available in from our website (www.dicraft.co.za). You can also make your own (see page 13).*

To save time, the separate waterlily leaf is prepared at the same time as the frog on the waterlily leaf.

If you do not have a full-colour cloth print of the frog and the separate waterlily leaf, prepare these as detailed on page 13.

Cut a block of interfacing the same size as the fabric print. Set the iron on a medium setting with the steam off. Place the fabric print right side down on the ironing board. Place the interfacing block shiny or rough (glue) side down on the wrong side of the print. Iron the interfacing, so it bonds well with the fabric and ensure the edges do not lift off the print.

Use a pair of small, sharp scissors and carefully cut out the frog on the leaf shape and the waterlily leaf (if you are making the waterlily) as neatly as possible. The interfacing backing prevents fraying along the edge.

Insert the water-soluble fabric in a 15 cm (6 in) hoop. Place the shapes, interfacing side down (right side up) on the water-soluble fabric.

Leave a 2 cm (3/4 in) space between the shapes. Use a water-soluble multipurpose glue stick (similar to the ones used at school) to lightly glue the shapes to the water-soluble fabric.

Hint: *If too much glue is used, it dissolves the water-soluble fabric. Simply lift the shape and place elsewhere on the fabric.*

Start with the waterlily leaf on which the frog is sitting: Thread up with the brown Baked Earth thread and use a stem stitch or buttonhole/blanket stitch along the edge. Start at the rounded base of the leaf alongside the frog and work in a counter-clockwise direction (or clockwise if you are left-handed). Stitch around the edge of the leaf. Use the same thread and make a few straight stitches to form the centre of the leaf underneath the frog. End off with a few back stitches at the back.

Embroider the frog: Change to the grey thread and attach a black bead for the eye. Use 4 or 5 stitches to secure well. Use a split or back stitch along the raw edge of the shape. Continue around the outline of the frog using the same stitch. Outline the bottom edge of the legs in the same way and add a few straight stitches on the leaf (beneath the frog) to form the darker shadows.

Use stab stitches to add the dark shadows on the front leg and the tiny stripes on the body.

Change to the green thread and use French knots (2 wraps) to form the toes. Use a tiny straight stitch to form the mouth. Outline the top edge of the front leg in the same green thread and back or split stitch.

Cut out the shape leaving a 10 mm (½ in) edge of water soluble fabric.

Place the shape in a bowl of water for four or five minutes. Remove and allow the shape to dry on a towel or dishcloth.

Align the shape with that on the main design, overlapping the waterlily petals as these will be worked on top later. Use the same brown thread and tiny stab stitches in the centre of the leaf (beneath the frog) to anchor the shape to the design. Use a gentle tension so the leaf does not fold up. Allow the outer edges to be free. Use the same thread and a small stab stitch beneath the frog's mouth to secure the head to the background.

Waterlily

Nymphaea capensis

The Nymphaea *genus include the waterlily, Egyptian lotus and pond lilies, beautiful ornamental aquatic plants named after the Greek goddess Nymphe. Water lilies are found in most parts of the world, in Australia, India, Egypt, Southern Africa, and the USA, and there are more than 50 species world wide. A beautiful, sometimes fragrant, ornamental plant ideal for garden ponds, ranging in colour from blue to pink, red, yellow and white, some are day and others night-opening. The blue or Egyptian lotus* (Nymphaea caerulea) *was revered by the ancient Egyptians for thousands of years. The* Nymphaea capensis *or Cape blue waterlily found in Southern and Eastern Africa and depicted here is a bright blue, day-blooming waterlily closely resembling the Egyptian lotus, with floating leaves of up to 35 cm (14 in) in diameter*

Hint: *This lily is ideal for embellishing wall quilts or trinket boxes or used to create a small, framed picture on a 28 count evenweave fabric. The raised, rounded shape and the beautiful shade of blue will certainly be an interesting focal point.*

Note: *Pre-printed full-colour panels with the embroidery shapes, including the waterlily leaf, are available from our website (www.dicraft.co.za). To make your own, see page 13.*

REQUIREMENTS

Cloth print of waterlily leaf
Yellow tipped stamens from cake decorating store
20 x 20 cm medium-weight iron-on interfacing
20 x 20 cm water-soluble fabric
Sharp 2B or 3B pencil
Water-soluble multipurpose glue stick (similar to the ones used at school)

CHAMELEON THREADS

Pure silk: Arctic Blue no 5
Stranded cotton: Baked Earth no 7, Moss no 54
Use 1 strand of thread unless otherwise specified

DI VAN NIEKERK'S RIBBONS

Silk: 13-mm no 77, no 63

STITCHES

Straight/stab stitch, stem stitch or blanket/buttonhole stitch, French knot, back or split stitch, ribbon stitch and overcast stitch

NEEDLES

Needles: Use a no 9 or no 10 crewel needle for one strand of thread
Use the no 18 chenille needle for the 13-mm ribbon

If you do not have a cloth print of the waterlily leaf, prepare one as detailed on page 13 and iron onto interfacing as detailed for the frog (see page 115). Use a pair of small sharp scissors and carefully cut out the interfacing-backed leaf.

Insert the water-soluble fabric in a 15 cm (6 in) hoop. Place the leaf on the water-soluble fabric and lightly glue in position with the glue stick. Thread up with the brown thread and, using a stem stitch or blanket/buttonhole stitch, work along the edge. Start at the rounded base of the leaf and work in a counter-clockwise direction (or clockwise if you are left handed). Stitch around the edge of the leaf. Use the same thread and make a few straight stitches to form the centre of the leaf. End off with a few back stitches at the back.

Hint: *If too much glue is used when gluing a cloth image to water-soluble fabric, it dissolves the water-soluble fabric. Simply lift the shape and place elsewhere on the fabric.*

Cut out the leaf leaving a 10 mm (½ in) edge of water soluble fabric. Place the shape in a bowl of water for four or five minutes. Remove and allow to dry on a towel or dishcloth.

Align the leaf with that on the design overlapping the water lily petals as these will be made on top later. Use the green thread and tiny stab stitches in the centre of the leaf to anchor the shape to the design. Use a gentle tension so the leaf does not fold up. Allow the outer edges to be free.

Make the cream leaves next. Thread up with the cream ribbon and use a ribbon stitch to form each leaf. Work from inside the edge of the blue petals outwards – the blue petals will be added on top later. Thread up with the brown thread and use a blanket stitch to edge the ribbon leaf. Use a few straight/stab stitches at the sharp tips to secure the ribbon to the design.

Change to the blue ribbon and use ribbon stitch to make the four petals in the very back row (the petals that are almost covered by the stamens in the final design). Start 3 mm inside the edge of the yellow stamens and work outwards. Use the blue thread and edge the petals in blanket stitch as before, anchoring the petals to the design with straight stitch.

Work the second back row of petals (there are three) on top of the four just made. Edge and anchor with the blue thread as before.

Add the yellow stamens next. Fold a small bunch of yellow stamens in half. Use small, sharp embroidery scissors and cut a small hole in the background fabric (through the backing fabric too) just beneath the blue ribbon petals. Take care not to cut the ribbon. Insert the folded stamens into the hole, and pull gently into place from the back. Use the green thread and attach the folded section to the back of the work. Use the same thread and overcast stitch to anchor the stamens on the right side of the work.

Make the five front petals. These petals can be made in ribbon stitch as for the back petals. You will need to work from the base of the waterlily upwards towards the yellow stamens, stitching through all the layers. Edge the petals in blanket stitch as before.

Alternatively, you can use ribbon appliqué for the front petals, making separate ribbon appliqué shapes that are only secured in place afterwards. With this method it is not necessary to stitch the ribbon through the folded stamens.

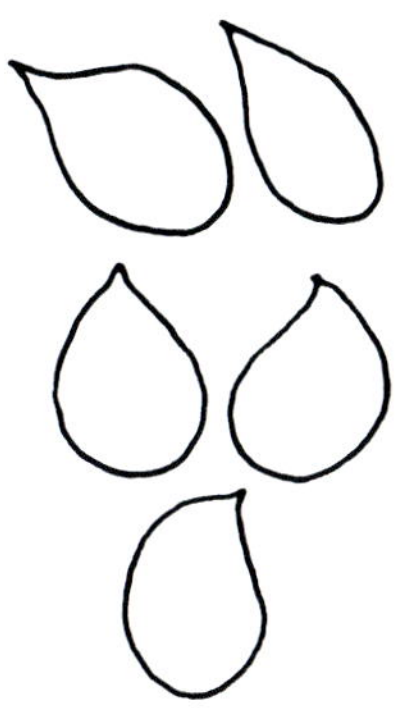

Trace the five petals above on the smooth non-fusible side (not on the shiny or rough) side of the interfacing. Use a soft, sharp 2B or 3B pencil and trace each shape. Cut out the interfacing shapes leaving an edge of about 2 mm.

Place the length of ribbon (any side up) on the ironing board. Set the iron on a medium setting with the steam off. (A dry iron is essential.) Place an interfacing shape pencil side up (shiny or rough side down) on top of the blue silk ribbon. Press each interfacing petal onto the ribbon, so the heat bonds it well. Do the same for all the shapes and take care not to scorch the ribbon.

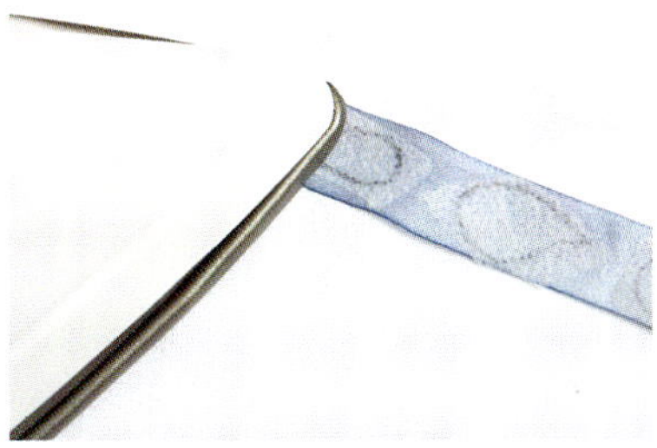

Cut out each petal along the pencil line as neatly as possible with small, sharp embroidery scissors. Insert the water-soluble fabric in a 15 cm (6 in) hoop. Place the five petals right side up on the water-soluble fabric leaving a 5 mm (¼ in) space between them. Use water-soluble multipurpose glue to lightly glue them to the water-soluble fabric.

Thread up with the blue thread. Start at the rounded base with a knot. Use a blanket stitch along the edge. At the sharp end of the shape, use the same thread and a few straight stitches to form the darker tips. End off by running the needle under the blanket stitches at the back.

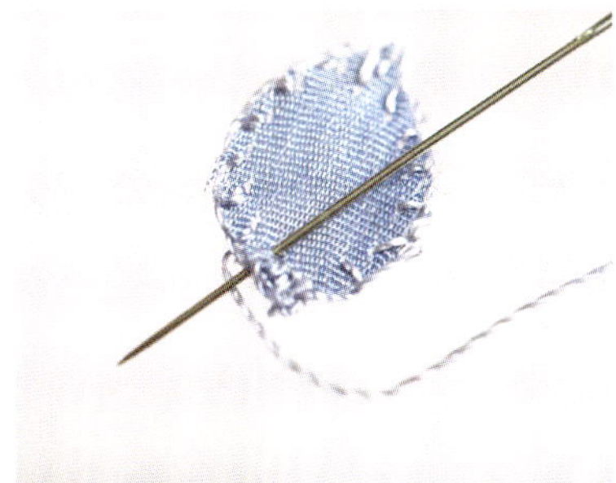

Cut out the shapes 3 mm away from the edge of the petal. Place shapes in a bowl of water for half a minute. Remove and allow the shapes to dry on a towel or dishcloth. Attach the petals over the stamens and back petals and secure in place with the blue thread. Make tiny stab stitches, at the base of each shape, allowing the outer and top edges to be free. Overlap the petals as shown.

PANEL FIFTEEN

Beetles

Mouse

Protea

Beetles

Order Coleoptera

Coleoptera *comes from the Greek words* koleos *meaning* sheath or shield, *and* ptera *meaning* wing. *Beetles are the largest order in the animal kingdom, with over 350 000 species. Dung beetles (the well-known scarab beetle being one of them) play a valuable role in improving soil structure. Some beetles are brightly coloured, some are green, others are yellow and black imitating wasps, and some are black to suit their nocturnal habits. Ladybirds, small rounded beetles with shiny shields dotted in bright colours from yellow to red are said to bring you luck if they land on you. They are also a real bonus in any garden as they feed on pests such as aphids and mites.*

CHAMELEON THREADS
Pure silk: Forest Green no 32, Egg yolk no 28, Knysna Forest no 3 Use one strand of thread throughout
DI VAN NIEKERK'S RIBBONS
Silk 2-mm no 36 for grass
RAJMAHAL ART SILK
Lagerfeld Ink no 25 or Charcoal no 29
METALLIC THREADS
Kreinik metallic blending filament no 32 Pearl
STITCHES
Stem or split stitch, back stitch, satin stitch, and straight/ stab stitch
NEEDLES
Use a no 9 or no 10 crewel needle for the threads and a no 22 or no 24 chenille for the 2-mm ribbon

Note: *The yellow and green beetles are made exactly the same way. Only the colours change. Use either the green or the yellow thread to complete the body.*

Outline the beetles' bodies and heads in the black thread and stem or split stitch. Fill in the black sections in stem stitch filling (rows of stem stitch made close together) for the longer black lines and straight and satin stitch for the shorter lines. Change to the yellow and then the green thread and fill in the yellow and green detail in satin stitch.

Work the heads next, filling in the outline in tiny French knots (two wraps) made close together.

The antennae are worked in straight stitch.

The legs are worked in back stitch for the folded legs and pistil stitch or straight stitch for the straight ones.

Thread up with the Pearl metallic thread and make French knots (two wraps) to form the eyes.

Thread up with the thin green ribbon and use a twisted straight stitch to form the tufts of grass. The ground is embroidered in seeding stitch and the light green thread.

Hint: *Use the water-soluble technique to make these beetles for scrapbook pages or cards. Trace the bodies onto white fabric, cut out and place water-soluble fabric in a 15 cm (6 in) hoop. Embroider as shown here. Cut out the shapes leaving a half centimetre edge and place in a bowl of water for a few minutes to dissolve the film. Allow to dry and attach to your page or card with acid-free glue. Draw in the legs and antennae with a black fine-liner.*

Mouse

Rhabdomys pumilio

Mouse *is an ancient Sanskrit word meaning* thief *which probably refers more to city mice than field mice! The four-striped field mouse* (Rhabdomys pumilio) *depicted here, has four long black stripes down its back, lives in the wild and feeds mainly on seeds, grain, plants, vegetables and insects. It helps to pollinate many protea species, transferring pollen that clings to its head when it feeds from one protea plant to another. This endearing little field mouse makes tunnels in grass, lives in nests of leaves and grass and moves on the ground rather than climbing trees and shrubs or burrowing holes. It is a diurnal animal, foraging for food during the day.*

Hint: *This cute little mouse is just perfect to peep over a strip of ribbon or paper on a card or scrapbooking page. Embroider as shown below, cut out and attach with stitches or acid-free glue. Allow the front feet to lie over a strip of organza or silk ribbon or fabric.*

REQUIREMENTS
20 x 20 cm soft white polycotton or cotton Fray Stop or anti-fray agent #26 wire
CHAMELEON THREADS
Pure silk: Rose no 64, Scottish Heather no 68 Stranded cotton: Baked Earth no 7 Use 1 strand of thread throughout
RAJMAHAL ART SILK
No 25 Lagerfeld Ink or no 29 Charcoal
METALLIC THREADS
Kreinik metallic blending filament no 32 Pearl
STITCHES
Stem stitch, French knot, straight/stab stitch, long and short stitch, stem stitch filling
NEEDLES
Use the fine no 9 or no 10 crewel needle

Note: *The mouse is made separately, cut out and placed so it fits behind the protea detailed in the next section.*

If you don't have a printed shape, trace the mouse below in the centre of the white fabric with a sharp HB or 2B pencil. Trace all the direction lines and detail on the mouse as neatly as possible to ensure a good finish. The tabs beneath the body will be inserted under the protea later. There is no need to embroider them as they will be hidden under the flower. Insert the fabric in a 15 cm (6 in) hoop. Pull the fabric taut as a drum and tighten the hoop. Roll up the corners and pin or tack out of the way so they don't hinder you as you work.

Thread up with the brown thread and outline the ears, head, nose, edge of the front legs and toes and rounded outside edge of the body in fine stem stitch. Remember to start inside the shape so the knot is not on the edge.

Change to the black thread and form the eyes in tiny stem stitches. Use the Pearl metallic thread and form a French knot (two wraps) in the centre of the eyes. Use the same metallic

thread and tiny straight/stab stitches to fill in the light part of the ears. Change to the pink thread and use stem or straight stitch to fill in the pink part of the ears.

Use the brown thread and fill in the head in long and short stitch. Work from the tip of the nose and edge of the head upwards to the top of the head fanning out (radiating) the first few stitches on the nose.

Hint: Follow the stitch direction lines for a natural finish. Stitch over the outline stitches for a raised edge and go back to fill the gaps each time. Make the stitches quite long (about 3 to 6-mm in length) for a smooth texture. Take care not to stitch on the black stitches of the eye.

Use the same thread and stem stitch filling (rows of stem stitch close together) to form the curved lines of the front legs. Keep the stitches small and curved as for the ears. Fill in the feet in long and short stitch (if using the pre-printed mouse in full colour, there is no need to cover the feet with stitches). The toes are formed in tiny straight/ stab stitches. The body is filled in the same thread and long and short stitch. Work from the leg outwards and stitch over the outline stitches for a raised edge.

Use the anti-fray agent around the edge of the shape. There is no need to wait for it to dry. Cut out the mouse, leaving a small seam that will be neatened in the next step. Remember not to cut off the tabs by mistake. Once you are holding the mouse, cut neatly along the edge leaving the tabs intact. Set aside and make the tail.

Cut a 10 cm (4 in) length of the wire. Fold in half and loosely wind the wires around each other allowing the folded section to form a rounded loop. Use nail clippers or wire cutters to cut the raw ends at an angle so one end is shorter than the other to form a sharp tip. Line up the sharp ends with the tip of the tail on the main design. Bend the wire to form the curved tail, working over the leaf. Note how the folded end fits over the mouse and protea on the design. These shapes are attached over the tail in the next step. Thread up with 1 strand of pink and 1 strand of brown thread (about 60 cm in length) on the same needle. Start with a knot at the long end and use three or four overcast stitches to secure the looped wire in place, so this section of the tail is attached on top of the protea on the design.

Wrap the tail: Bend the wire straight again so it is easy to wrap. Lift the secured wire up and wrap the thread tightly around the wire pulling it taut so the wraps sit snugly around the wire.

At the other end insert the needle into the previous wraps and pull taut. Anchor the tip of the tail to the design with overcast stitches. Complete by adding a straight/stab stitch to form a pointed tail. Bend the tail in shape.

Attach the mouse over the tail and protea. Line up the shape with that on the design. Use the brown thread and tiny stab stitches to attach the mouse along the edge, under the ears and on the tabs (seams.) Leave the ears, feet and top of the head free. Fill the shape from the top of the head with toy filling or shredded wadding, so a nice, rounded shape is formed. Use the same thread and stitch to close the gap, allowing the ears and feet to be free. The feet will lie on top of the protea later. Thread up with the grey thread and use long, straight stitches to form the whiskers.

Protea compacta

Common name: Bot River Sugarbush, Bot River Protea, Botrivierprotea

Protea is a genus consisting of well over 100 species of beautiful evergreen flowering shrubs and small trees found in the Cape Floral region in South Africa. Protea compacta *is a tall, dense, evergreen shrub reaching heights of up to 3,5 m. The cup-shaped protea flower with its striking rose pink bracts or leaves that open to show its pearly flowers it is an attractive and popular cut flower that lasts for 10 to 20 days in a vase. It grows in the Caledon and Bredasdorp region and is also found at the coast as far as Knysna on the Garden Route. This is a good shrub to grow in coastal gardens for hedges or eye-catching focal points, flowering in winter to spring.* Protea compacta *prefers a low altitude from 0 to 200 metres, grows in well-drained, sandy soil in open, sunny spots. It is drought resistant and best planted on a hill or sloping site, so the water drains off without delay. It does not mind the wind, attracts butterflies to the garden and is pollinated by birds and mice.*

Hint: *This unusual flower is ideal to embellish ethnic wall hangings and quilts, on cloth-covered boxes or as a small, framed embroidered picture for someone special.*

REQUIREMENTS
20 x 20 cm soft white polycotton or cotton Sharp 2B or 3B pencil or blue pen with water-soluble ink Fray Stop or anti-fray agent 15 x 15 cm medium-weight iron-on interfacing 20 x 20 cm water-soluble fabric Water-soluble multipurpose glue stick (similar to the ones used at school) #28 wire Small piece of toy filling
CHAMELEON THREADS
Pure silk: Emerald no 101, Daffodil no 23, Spilt Milk no 77, Rose no 64 Stranded cotton: Baked Earth no 7, Golden Green no 36 Use 1 strand of thread unless otherwise specified
DI VAN NIEKERK'S RIBBONS
Silk: 13-mm no 45 and Organza: 7-mm no 15 and 124.
STITCHES
Straight/stab stitch, couching, buttonhole – long and short, buttonhole/blanket stitch, stem stitch, long and short stitch, fly stitch, ribbon stitch, French knot
NEEDLES
Use the fine no 9 or no 10 crewel needle for the threads Use the no 18 chenille needle for the 7-mm ribbon

Hint: *Pre-printed full-colour panels with the different embroidery shapes are available in from our website (www.di-craft.co.za). It is certainly is much easier to embroider on a colour-printed image than a line-tracing.*

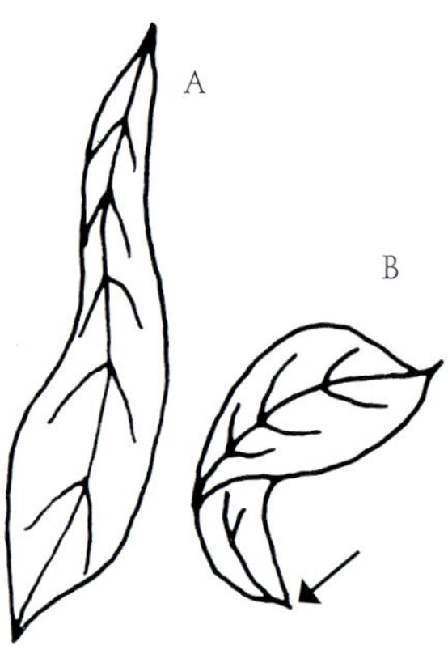

If you don't have printed shapes, trace the 2 leaves and the oval-shaped protea centre below in the centre of the white fabric with a sharp HB or 2B pencil. Trace all the direction lines and detail as neatly as possible to ensure a good finish. Insert the fabric in a 15 cm (6 in) hoop. Pull the fabric

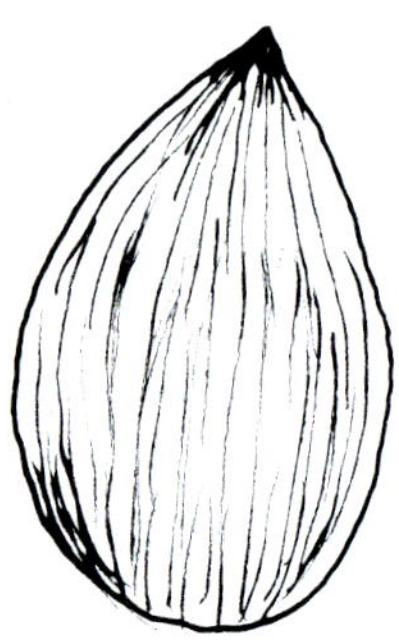

taut as a drum and tighten the hoop. Roll up the corners and pin or tack out of the way, so they don't hinder you as you work.

Use the #28 wire for the bent leaf A. There is no need for wire along the edge of leaf B, as it is not lifted off the design. Insert 2 or 3 cm of the wire to the back of the work at the base of the leaf (indicated with an arrow) Tape the wire in place with masking tape, so it is out of the way and won't be caught on your threads as you embroider. Remember to start inside the shape so the knot is not on the edge. Couch the wire in place along the outside of the leaf every 3 mm or so with the dark green thread. The fold line on the leaf does not have wire; this fold is formed with stem stitch later. To form a neat edge, angle the needle close to the wire, over, and back into the same hole again. Insert the wire to the back again, cut and tape in place as before. Use a buttonhole stitch to cover the wire (see buttonhole stitch over wire on page 153). The fold line on the leaf is outlined in the same green thread and stem stitch

Outline the edge of leaf B (this leaf does not have a wired edge) in the same thread and long and short buttonhole stitch. Change to 2 strands of thread and fill in both leaves. Fill in leaf A with long and short stitch and insert the needle along the central vein each time. Follow the direction lines on the leaf, so the leaf appears to be folded and stitch over the stem stitch on the folded line.

Hint: *Remember to slant the stitch towards the base of the leaf each time for a natural finish.*

Do the same for leaf B. Form the veins on top of the leaves in the Golden Green thread and fly or straight stitch.

Embroider the oval centre. Thread up with 1 strand of the pale yellow and 1 strand of the white thread on one needle. Outline the edge in stem stitch first. Remember to start inside the shape so the knot is not on the edge. Fill the shape with long, straight stitches or long and short stitch. Use long stitches (about 1 to 2 cm or ¼ to ½ in long and insert the needle into the same hole each time to form the sharp tip. Change to the brown thread and add a few brown straight stitches in-between the paler ones to form shadows. Add a few pink straight stitches at the tip.

Apply anti-fray agent along the edges of the three shapes. Cut out leaf A, cutting close to the edge but taking care not to cut the stitches. Cut out leaf B and the oval centre neatly along the edge, taking care not to cut the stitches.

Insert leaf A at the base of the protea. Make a small hole on the main design just beneath the protea with the sharp point of your small embroidery scissors or use a no 16 or 18 chenille needle. Insert the wires of the leaf into this hole until it lies snugly against the fabric. Bend the wires towards the rear so that they are positioned under the leaf at the back of the work. Use the brown thread to secure the wire to the back of the work. Cut off excess wire so that the threads don't catch on the loose ends. Use the same brown thread and straight stitches at the tip of the leaf to secure the leaf over the mouse's tail.

Align leaf B with the leaf on the design and attach with the same thread and tiny straight stitches along the base and tip of the leaf. The prepared protea will overlap this leaf later.

Thread up with the organza ribbon and form the thick green stem of the protea with two straight stitches overlapping each other. Work over the leaves and a few millimetres into the protea bracts (petal leaves) on the design. These will be placed on top later. Thread up with the brown thread and form the knobbles on the green organza stem in French knots and straight/stab stitch

The pink protea bracts (leaf/petals) are made separately with silk ribbon ironed onto iron-on interfacing to prevent fraying and to stabilize the ribbon bracts, and then attached beneath and on top of the oval centre.

Use a soft, sharp 2B or 3B pencil and trace the shapes above as neatly as possible onto the smooth, non-fusible side (not on the shiny or rough side) side of interfacing. Cut out the interfacing shapes about a millimetre from the edge. Don't cut on the pencil line yet.

Hint: *To prevent fraying, only cut along the pencil line once the interfacing has been ironed onto the ribbon.*

Place the length of ribbon (any side up) on the ironing board. Set the iron on a medium setting with the steam off. (A dry iron is essential.)

Place an interfacing shape pencil side up (shiny or rough side down) on top of the pink silk ribbon. Press each interfacing petal onto the ribbon so the heat bonds it well. Repeat for all the shapes and take care not to scorch the ribbon. Check that each interfacing shape adheres well to the ribbon, and that it does not lift at the edges.

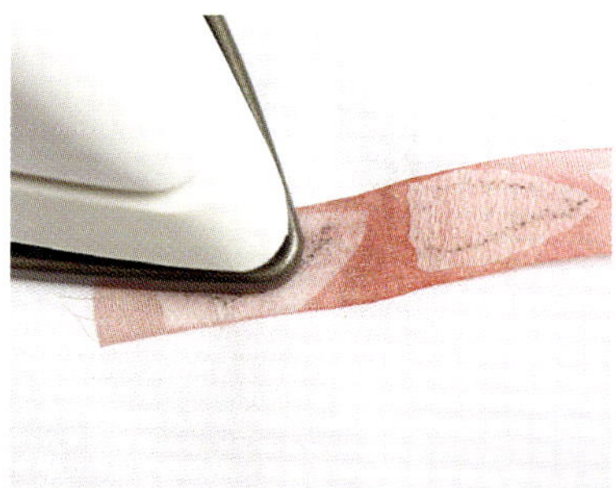

Hint: *If you find your iron has glue residue because you ironed on the wrong side of a petal by mistake, clean with a tube of hot-iron cleaner available from most supermarkets. Follow the manufacturer's instructions.*

Cut out each pink shape along the pencil line as neatly as possible with small, sharp embroidery scissors. Insert the water-soluble fabric in a 15 cm (6 in) hoop. Place the 22 pink shapes, pencil (interfacing) side down (right side up) on the water-soluble layer. Leave 5 mm between the shapes and lightly glue to the water-soluble fabric with a water-soluble multipurpose glue stick (similar to the ones used at school).

Hint: *If too much glue is used, it dissolves the water-soluble fabric. Simply lift the shape and place elsewhere on the fabric.*

Thread up with the brown thread. Start at the rounded base with a knot. Use a blanket stitch along the edge and work anti-clockwise (clockwise if you are left-handed) around the shape. At the sharp end of the shape use the same thread and a few straight

stitches to form the darker tips. End off by running the needle under the blanket stitches at the back. Do the same for all the shapes.

Hint: *Start with a knot at the long end, but ensure the knot is never along the edge of the shape. Always start a short distance inside the shape and make a running stitch to reach the outer edge again. This way the knot is not visible when the shape is attached to the design.*

Cut out the shapes a few millimetres away from the edge of the petal. Place shapes in a bowl of water for half a minute. Remove and allow the shapes to dry on a towel or dishcloth.

Hint: *If the shapes are left in the water only a short while, they remain sticky and have more body. Once the shapes are dry they are bent and retain their shape. Every now and then, while they are drying, move the shapes so they don't stick to the towel or dishcloth. The shapes curl up slightly and this is what makes them look so real.*

First attach the shapes that need to lie under the oval centre at the tip of the protea. Choose six of the shortest bracts and attach in place with the brown thread and tiny stab stitches at the base of each shape. Add a few tiny straight stitches along the tips to stabilize, allowing the outer edges to be free.

Place the oval centre on top of the protea on the main design. Overlap the base of the pink bracts that have just been attached and align the sharp tip and rounded base so the oval shape is in the centre of the flower. Use a matching thread and work tiny stab stitches every centimetre or so to attach the oval to the design, but leave the sharp tip open. Use toy filling or shredded batting to fill the oval shape at the open tip to form a fat, rounded centre. Close the sharp tip with the pink thread and a few straight stitches.

Use the pale mushroom shade of organza ribbon and ribbon stitches to form a lining. This lining will support and elevate the pink bracts that are placed on top in the next step. Refer to the picture of the completed protea and place the ribbon stitches so they lie underneath each pink bract. Stitch alongside and on the base of the oval centre. Work from the top down to the base, overlapping the stitches as shown. Take care not to stitch over the section of the oval centre that is visible on the protea.

Attach the remaining pink bracts. Refer to the photograph of the completed protea and work from the top downwards to the base. Use the brown thread and stab stitch along the base of each petal, attaching one petal at a time.

Overlap the petals as shown and use tiny straight stitches at the tips of some bracts to stabilize. At the base of the protea, use the same brown thread and straight stitches to add more texture on top of the green stem and between the bracts.

Use the same brown thread and stab stitches to anchor the edges of the petals along the green leaf so they appear to be folded under the protea.

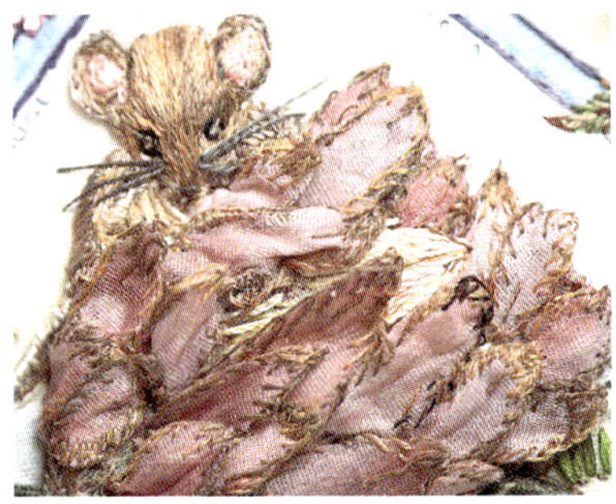

Use the blunt end of the needle to free the feet of the mouse, so they will lie on top of the protea. Use the same stab stitch to tuck the pink bracts along the edge of the protea as before. Finally, bend some of the bracts towards you, so the oval centre is more exposed.

PANEL SIXTEEN

Sunflowers

Coreopsis

Butterfly

Sunflower

Helianthus annuus

The genus name Helianthus *comes from the Greek words* helios *meaning* sun *and* anthos *meaning* flower. *Native to North America, the sunflower is the state flower of Kansas. This tall, hardy, annual or perennial has been cultivated for centuries by the North American Indians and was introduced to Europe in the 16th century. The sunflower is produced for its seeds as an oilseed plant all over the world and to feed livestock, as bird seed, for cooking, cosmetics and soap oil, and as a healthy snack or for use in salads, breads and cakes. The showy petals, (called ray flowers) are bright yellow although some varieties are orange, rust, maroon red and ivory with a dark brown centre containing hundreds of tiny flowers grouped together. It is one of the world's top selling cut flowers. Flowerheads are up to 30 cm in diameter. Ideal for the garden, the sunflower attracts birds, bees, squirrels and butterflies. In the bud stage, sunflowers turn to follow the sun. They like fertile, well-drained soil and full sun.*

Hint: *These bright and cheerful flowers are ideal for the embellishment of cushions, quilts, or trinket boxes. Instead of making separate leaves as shown below, embroider all the leaves directly on the background fabric for jerseys, handbags, a pocket or bodice of a dress.*

REQUIREMENTS

20 x 20 cm soft white polycotton or cotton
Fray-stop or any good anti-fray agent

CHAMELEON THREADS

Pure silk: Charcoal no 15, Green Olives no 97, Pine Needles no 61, Egg Yolk no 28
Stranded cotton: Baked Earth no 7
Use 1 strand of thread unless otherwise specified

DI VAN NIEKERK'S RIBBONS

Silk ribbon: 4-mm no 82, no 95, no 99

STITCHES

Straight/stab stitch, straight stitch – twisted, couching, ribbon stitch, buttonhole – long and short, long and short stitch, satin stitch, satin stitch – padded, detached chain/lazy daisy, French knot, single knotted stitch, stem stitch, back stitch

NEEDLES

Use the no 8 crewel needle for 2 strands of thread and the no 9 or no 10 for one strand of thread
Use the no 20 or no 22 chenille for the 4-mm ribbon

For scrapbooking and card-making, embroider the sunflowers on a block of organza fabric, stretch and mount the organza block to attach to your page or card with acid-free glue.

Note: *The sunflower is made in two parts. The yellow petals (ray flowers) are embroidered directly on the main design and the brown centres are made separately and attached on top of the ribbon. Two of the leaves are made separately as well and then attached to the background.*

Trace the four shapes in the middle of the white fabric block. Use a sharp HB pencil and trace in all the detail, as this will guide you later as you work. Insert in a 15 cm (6 in) hoop.

Work the leaf shapes first. There is no need for wire around the edge of these leaves as they do not need to be bent into shape. Thread up with 2 strands of the olive green thread and work in long and short buttonhole stitch to form a neat edge. Start at the sharp tip with a detached chain and continue down the one half of the leaf in long and short buttonhole stitch.

Start at the sharp tip again and outline the other half as before. Fill in the leaf with long and short or satin stitch and insert the needle along the central vein each time. Form the central veins of the leaves in the green or brown thread and stem stitch or tiny horizontal satin stitches made close together.

Hint: *Remember to slant the stitch towards the base of the leaf each time for a natural finish.*

Form the brown centres next. Thread up with 1 strand of black and 1 strand of brown thread on one needle. Embroider the 2 dark circles (the outer and inner circles) in French knots (one wrap) and make the knots close together for a dense texture.

Use 2 strands of the brown thread as before to form the light brown circle.

Apply anti-fray around the edges of the shapes and cut out the shapes leaving a small edge. Once you are holding the shape in your hand, cut close to the edge of the stitches, cutting away all the white fabric but taking care not to damage the stitches. Set shapes aside for later use.

Hint: *Run a green or brown permanent fabric marker along the edge of the leaves and centres to hide any white edge.*

Thread up with the green silk ribbon and use a twisted straight stitch to form the stems. Work from the outside edge towards the sunflower and insert the needle to the back at the brown centre. The centre and yellow petals will be added on top later. Keep a loose tension and couch in place every one or two centimetres with the lighter green thread. End off at the back. Using the same ribbon and method, repeat for the other sunflower. Form the green calyx beneath the yellow petals of both sunflowers in the same ribbon and detached chain/lazy daisy with a long anchoring stitch. Start on top of the yellow petals and work outwards. The yellow petals will be added on top later.

Thread up with two strands of the lighter green thread and use a padded satin stitch to form the two remaining leaves on the design. Outline the edge of each leaf first in back or stab stitch taking care to keep the tooth like shape. Work from the centre vein outwards, and fill in the leaf in satin stitch. Stitch over the outline to form a raised edge.

Hint: *Remember to slant the stitch towards the base of the leaf each time for a natural finish.*

Change to the darker olive thread and form the dark veins and stems of the leaves in stem stitch.

The yellow petals (ray flowers) are embroidered directly on the background fabric. Use the no 99 yellow ribbon and work the bottom petals that will lie underneath the others first. Work from the brown centre outwards and use a ribbon stitch for each petal. Thread up with the yellow thread and make a straight stitch or detached chain/lazy daisy at the tip of each petal to secure and stabilize the stitch to the background. Thread up with the no 95 silk ribbon and complete the top layer of petals in the same manner, working from the brown centre outwards. Use the same yellow thread and the same stitch at the tips to stabilize the petals and to add an interesting effect.

Place the embroidered brown centres on top of the yellow petals (ray flowers) and secure in place with the brown thread and tiny stab stitches.

Use the no 99 silk ribbon and form the petals lying on top of the brown centres in loose, puffed ribbon stitch (push the ribbon up to form a loose, curly stitch, before piercing it and taking the needle to the back of the work).

Hint: *For an interesting effect, one or two petals can be formed in single knotted stitch and then cut so the tips of the petals are released from the background.*

Finally, attach the two loose leaves to the design in matching green thread and tiny stab stitches along the base and tip of the leaves.

Coreopsis tinctoria

Common name: Golden tickseed, calliopsis

Native to the Americas, this hardy annual is an exceptional bloomer and with its bright clusters of flowers in colours ranging from yellow to orange, pink, maroon, red and bronze, it is a most useful garden plant. Reaching 30 to 90 cm in height, Coreopsis tinctoria *is easy to grow, is self-seeding and useful for areas with poor soil conditions. Drought resistant, it needs well-drained soil in full sun or semi-shade and is often found in ditches along roadsides. Its bright colours attract butterflies, bees and birds to the garden. It will not grow in heavy clay soil.*

Hint: *Make this basket of flowers to add a special touch to a beautiful scrapbook page or card. Embroider on a square of fabric, stretch and mount and use an acid-free glue to attach to your paper. Stitch the design on quilts, cushions, clothing, and handbags or trinket boxes.*

REQUIREMENTS
Mill Hill frosted glass beads no 62044 3 medium (3 or 4-mm) necklace beads in pale cream, green or clear
CHAMELEON THREADS
Forest Green no 32, Peacock no 103, Goldrush no 37, Tropical green no 3 Stranded cotton: Baked Earth no 7 Use 1 strand of thread unless otherwise specified
DI VAN NIEKERK'S RIBBONS
Silk 4-mm no 80, 7-mm no 57
STITCHES
Woven filling stitch, stem stitch, straight/stab stitch, loop stitch, straight stitch – twisted, grab stitch, ribbon stitch, French knot
NEEDLES
Use the no 9 or no 10 crewel for one strand of thread and the no 10 for beading Use the no 18 chenille for the 7-mm ribbon and no 20 or no 22 chenille for the 4-mm ribbon

Work the basket first. Thread up with the forest green thread and use a woven filling-stitch to form the basket. Make the foundation stitches first. These are vertical straight stitches placed 4 mm apart. Start at the edge of the basket and space evenly, ending on the opposite edge of the basket. Work over the flowers and stem – these will be added on top later.

Use the same thread and woven filling stitch to fill the basket working from side to side, packing the rows close together to form a dense texture. Use the same thread and stem stitch along the underside of the basket to add the bottom rim. Do the same for the top rim, working over the flowers as before. Use the blue thread and horizontal straight/stab stitches to form the grains of the wooden shelf alongside and beneath the basket. Use a row of stem stitch beneath the green basket rim to add a shadow.

Form the thin stems of the green buds and orange flowers in the 4-mm green silk ribbon and twisted straight stitch. The rounded green buds are formed over beads to create the raised shapes. Thread up with the light green thread and attach a medium bead for each green bud on the design. Attach with 5 or 6 stitches, so the bead is anchored securely on the fabric.

Thread up with the 7-mm green ribbon and cover the bead in ribbon stitch. Insert the needle at an angle under the bead, so the ribbon fits snugly around the bead. Repeat several times, so the bead is covered.

Hint: *See Panel 1 page 18 for an illustration showing stitching over a bead.*

Use the 4-mm ribbon and a grab stitch at the base of the bud to form a rounded calyx. Complete the calyx (leaves at the base of the bud) in the same ribbon and straight stitch.

Form the orange petals in loop stitch. Thread up with the orange ribbon and form one loop for each petal working over a large tapestry needle or any similar object. Work from the centre of the flower outwards. Hold the previous loop in place, only moving the needle once the second loop is made. Thread up with the golden thread and use tiny stab stitches along the base of each petal to stabilize the loops. Use the same stab stitch to anchor some of the loops to the design along the folded edge of the ribbon.

Use the same thread and attach an orange bead in the centre of the flower. Use 2 or 3 anchoring stitches for each bead. Make a few tiny French knots (1 wrap) alongside the bead in the same golden thread. Finally, thread up with the brown thread and add a few brown French knots as before alongside the bead to form the shadows.

Note: *The flower on the shelf, hanging over the blue border, does not have a bead, as this flower is shown from the side.*

Butterfly

Butterfly order Lepidoptera

There are about 150 000 butterfly and moth species worldwide, both from the order Lepidoptera. *Butterflies are flying insects with large, beautiful, colourful wings that magnetize children and adults alike. The wings are colourful, owing to the loose powdery scales that rub off when touched. Like all insects, butterflies have six legs. Their long, thin body is divided into a head, a thorax and an abdomen and they have two knobbed antennae. Butterflies are a significant part of conservation, as they pollinate plants. They fly during the day and rest at night with their wings held erect. Many butterflies migrate to avoid cold winters.*

Hint: *Pre-printed wings in full colour, as I have used here, are available from our website (www.dicraft.co.za).*

REQUIREMENTS
Yellow metallic thread or blending filament (optional) Use 1 strand of thread unless otherwise specified 20 x 20 cm soft white polycotton or cotton Sharp HB or 2B pencil. #30 wire-white or green from cake decorating shops Brown or black stamen from cake decorating shops Fray Stop or anti-fray agent
CHAMELEON THREADS
Pure silk: Daffodil no 23 or Egg Yolk no 28 Charcoal no 15
RAJMAHAL ART SILK
No 25 Lagerfeld Ink or no 29 Charcoal
STITCHES
Straight/stab stitch, couching, buttonhole stitch, long and short stitch, satin stitch, French knot, pistil stitch, running stitch, stem stitch filling, stem stitch, split stitch, satin stitch – padded, overcast stitch
NEEDLES
Use no 9 or no 10 crewel for one strand of thread

Note: *The back (lowermost) wing is embroidered directly on the background fabric of the design. The two wings in front are made separately and attached to the design.*

Use the sharp pencil and carefully trace the two separate wings and veins in the centre of the block of white fabric. Place the block in a 15 cm (6 in) hoop.

Use the #30 wire for the wings. Insert 2 or 3 cm of the wire to the back of the work on the sharp point of the wing. Tape the wire in place with masking tape, so it is out of the way and won't be caught on your threads as you embroider. Couch the wire in place every 3 mm or so with the Rajmahal Art Silk thread. Use two strands of the same thread and a buttonhole stitch to cover the wire (see buttonhole stitch over wire in the stitch gallery) take the needle to the back before inserting it through the loop each time.

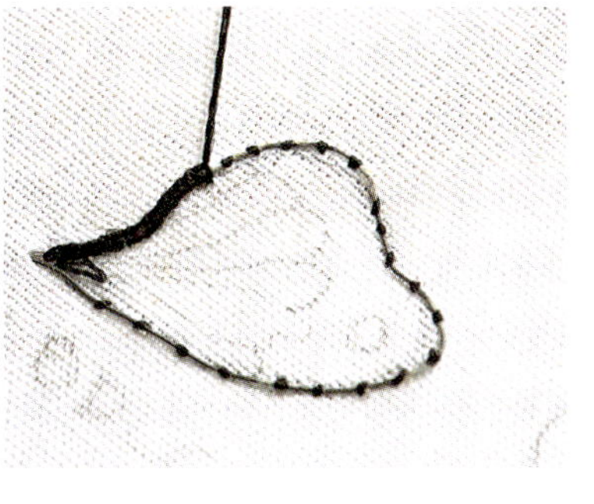

Hint: *First strip the plastic coating off the wire by holding the wire on a towel or dishcloth. Use the outer blunt edge of the old pair of scissors and run the scissors over the wire to strip the coating. This way the wire is finer and not too thick for the delicate wings.*

Use the same black thread and long and short stitch to form the black edge of the wings. Form the black veins in stem stitch.

Change to the yellow thread and fill in the yellow sections in stem stitch filling (rows of stem stitch made close together) for the larger sections and satin stitch or French knots for the smaller circles. Finally, use the yellow metallic thread (this is optional) and fill in the shiny yellow part at the top of the wing in stem stitch filling as before for highlights.

Work on the main design. Outline the backwing in one strand of charcoal thread in stem or split stitch.

Use the same thread and form the black edge in padded satin stitch stitching over the outline to form a raised edge. Fill in the black veins as before and the yellow sections in the same stitch used for the other two wings in the hoop.

Use the same charcoal thread and form the black head thorax and abdomen in French knots (one wrap) made close together. Change to one strand of the Rajmahal art silk thread and outline the body and head in fine stem or split stitch to neaten the edge. Use a straight stitch for the top part and pistil stitch for the bottom part of the leg.

Attach the stamen to form the antennae. Use a no 18 chenille needle (or the sharp tip of the small embroidery scissors) to make a small hole in the design. Insert the folded stamen in the hole. Alternatively, fold the stamen in half and thread the folded section through the eye of the needle. Take the needle to the back, working with a gentle tension. Hold onto the stamen tips on the right side, so they are not pulled through by mistake. Gently pull the stamen back to the front until you are happy with the length. Use the black thread and tiny overcast stitches at the base of the antennae to secure in place. Bend the folded string of the stamen at the back of the work and anchor in place with stab stitches. Cut off the excess string, ensuring that there are no raw ends to catch on your threads later.

Cut out the wings worked separately on the white fabric. Remove the tape and apply an anti-fray agent along the edge. Cut close to the edge with small sharp embroidery scissors. Be careful not to cut the stitches. Use a black laundry marker and draw along the edge to cover any white fabric that may be showing.

Make a small hole on the main design alongside the butterfly's body with the sharp point of your small embroidery scissors or use a size 16 or 18 chenille needle. Place the larger middle wing first by inserting the wire ends into the holes just formed. Bend the wire backwards at the back of the work, so it lies beneath the wing section, and attach in place with small stab stitches. Trim the wire edges, so that the threads don't catch on the raw ends.

Repeat for the remaining wing, attaching at the back as before. Use an overcast stitch on the wings at the side of the body in the black thread to secure them to the design so they are not too loose Allow the rounded edges to be free. Bend the wings into a pleasing shape.

PANEL SEVENTEEN

Corn poppies

Corn poppies

Papaver rhoeus

Also known as Flanders poppies, named after the famous poem of the First World War, "In Flanders Fields, the poppies blow, among the crosses row on row", *it is the Flower of Remembrance worn all over the world in honour of those who lost their lives in war. Native to Asia Minor, with many cultivated varieties, including double-flowered ones. Up to 90 cm tall, the delicate, single scarlet flowers grow above slender, hairy, branching stems with light-green, lobed leaves. The stigma is a flattened disk with eight or more rays. Self-seeding, they are quick and easy to grow, relishing loose, dry to moist, well-drained soil in full sun. They make good cut flowers if cut early in the morning. The seed is safe for human consumption (this poppy does not contain any opium). The seeds are used for baking, to make salad and cooking oils, and the red petals are used for syrups and dyes.*

REQUIREMENTS

Mill Hill petite glass beads no 42014-black
Soldering iron or stencil burner to seal edges of organza ribbon
20 x 20 cm soft white polycotton or cotton
Sharp HB and 2B or 3B pencil
Fray Stop or anti-fray agent

CHAMELEON THREADS

Pure silk: Pine Needles no 61, Granite no 105
Ruby Red no 65
Stranded cotton: Baked Earth no 7
Use 1 strand of thread unless otherwise specified

DI VAN NIEKERK'S RIBBONS

Silk: 4-mm no 35, no 54; 13-mm no 39
Organza: 38-mm no 39

RAJMAHAL ART SILK

No 25 Lagerfeld Ink or no 29 Charcoal

STITCHES

Straight/stab stitch, buttonhole – long and short, long and short stitch, ribbon stitch, loop stitch, running stitch, fly stitch, straight stitch – padded, straight stitch – twisted, satin stitch – padded, satin stitch, back stitch, stem stitch

NEEDLES

Use the fine no 9 or no 10 crewel needles for the threads and the no 10 for beading
Use the no 18 chenille needle for the 13-mm ribbon and no 20 to no 22 for the 4-mm ribbons

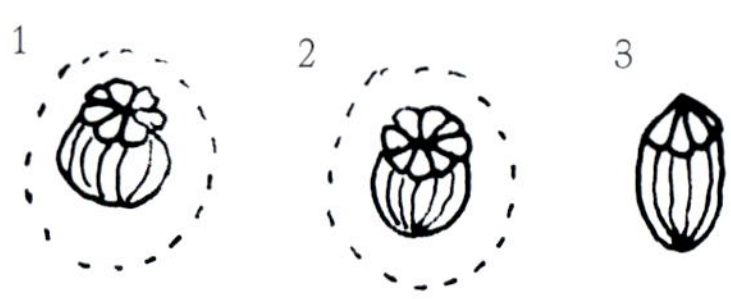

The 3 poppy centres (stigma) are made separately, then attached on top of the petals later. Trace the three shapes in the centre of the white fabric. Use a sharp HB pencil and draw in the wedges of the stigma and the direction lines as neatly as possible.

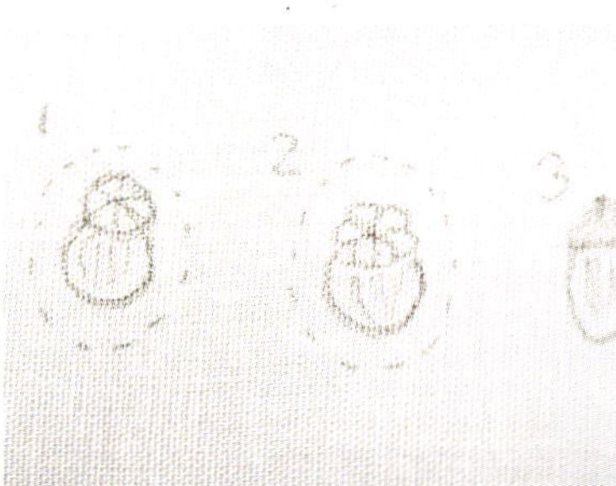

Number each shape and trace the dotted outside line on shapes 1 and 2. Insert in a 15 cm (6 in) hoop.

Thread up with 2 strands of the green thread and use a long and short buttonhole stitch to form a neat edge. Start beneath the yellow wedges and work along the pencil line in an anti-clockwise (clockwise if you are left-handed) direction to reach the yellow wedges on the opposite side. Fill in the green base in long and short stitch. Do the same for the remaining two shapes.

Hint: *Don't be too concerned about the neatness of the edge underneath the yellow wedges as this section will be covered later with yellow ribbon.*

Thread up with the yellow ribbon. Make a knot at the long end. Insert the needle into the green thread on

the wrong side, so the knot lies in the centre of the green part of the shape. This will serve as padding later. Insert needle and ribbon to the front of the work in the centre of the yellow wedges. Form a ribbon stitch for each wedge, working from the centre outwards each time. If necessary, make one ribbon stitch on top of the other, to form a thicker wedge. End off by stitching the tail to the back of the shape with the brown thread. Use the same brown thread and straight stitch between each wedge to form a dark shadow between the shapes. Do the same for the two other shapes. Set aside till later.

Hint: *It is better not to cut the centres out at this stage as they tend to get lost!*

Form the stems of the poppies. Use the 4-mm green ribbon and twisted straight stitch. Start at the base between the leaves and keep the tension quite loose, so the ribbon will form a nice curve once stitched in place with thread. Stitch over the poppies and leaf as these will be added on top later. Thread up with the green thread and use tiny stab stitches here and there to coax the ribbon stem into shape. Some of the stems will end in the centre of the poppies and the petals will be added on top of this stem. End off each time and start at the base of the stem and leaves again. To end off attach the tail of the ribbon at the back of the poppy with tiny stab stitches in the green thread. Change to the granite thread and use tiny stab stitches to form the hairs on the stem working from the stem outwards.

Note: *It is not necessary to form the stem leading to the open poppy no 3 on the far left at this stage. This stem will be made on top later once the red petal has been added.*

Form the leaves next. Thread up with two strands of the green thread and use a padded satin stitch to form each leaf. Outline the edge of each leaf first in back or stab stitch, taking care to keep the tooth-like shape. Work from the centre vein outwards, and fill in the leaf in satin stitch. Stitch over the outline to form a raised edge. Change to the Granite thread and form the dark veins in stem stitch and straight stitch. Use tiny stab stitches along the edge of the leaf to form the sharp tips.

Hint: *Remember to slant the stitch towards the base of the leaf each time for a natural finish.*

Form the little top bud next. Thread up with the 13-mm silk ribbon and use a padded straight stitch to work the pink bud. Use the green silk ribbon and a fly stitch along the edge of the bud to form the calyx.

Hint: *Make two fly stitches on top of each other to form a broader stitch. Thread up with the Granite thread and use tiny stab stitches to form the hairs along the edge.*

Now work the poppy petals. Trace the shapes on page 140 on the 38-mm organza ribbon. Use a soft 2B or 3B pencil so the lines will be visible. Draw the dotted lines (these will be the lines that will be gathered later) and number each shape exactly as shown. This way the numbers won't be visible once the poppy is made.

Cut out each shape along the pencil line. Use heat to seal the raw edges.

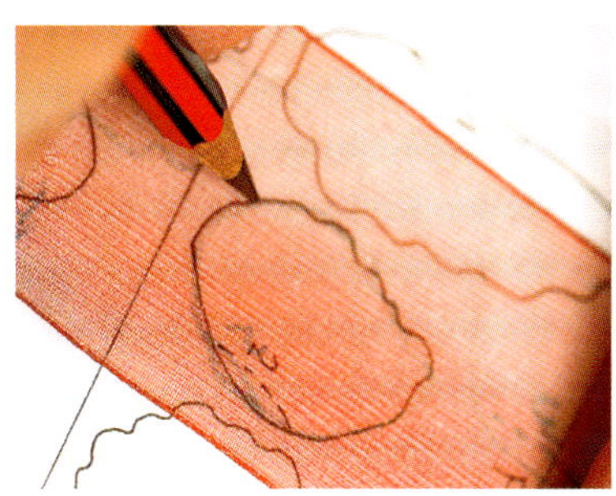

Practise with scrap pieces of ribbon first to become accustomed to the gentle contact necessary for this step. Too heavy a touch and the organza petal will melt and the shape becomes too small.

If this does happen, extra petals can be added to enlarge the poppy. Hold the petal in your free hand, pinching the edge with the marked dotted line and number between your thumb and forefinger. Use a heated soldering iron or stencil burner (read the manufacturer's instructions for the heating tool). Be careful not to burn yourself. Move the heated tool around the edges of the petal. It is not necessary to seal the edge that you are holding, as this side is gathered in the next step and attached to the fabric. Repeat for all 10 petals.

Hint: *This heat sealing method is ideal for neatening edges of organza stumpwork wings (or any organza shape) in future projects.*

Thread up with the Ruby Red thread and make a knot at the long end. Start with petal 1 of poppy 1 and work each petal in numerical order from 1 to 4. Use short running stitches along the dotted line on the unsealed edge. Pull to gather slightly and use

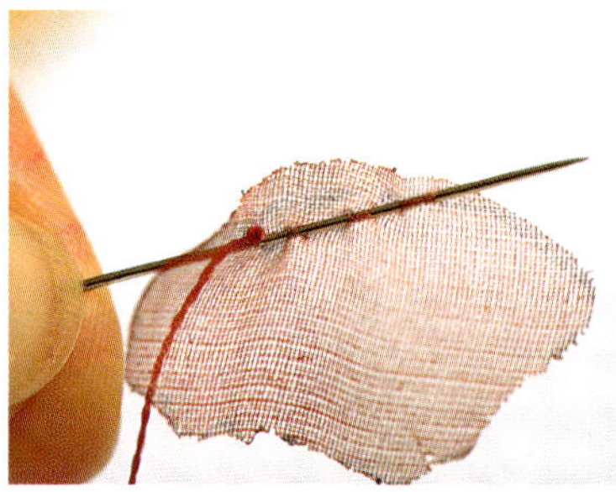

the same thread to attach the petal on top of the poppy centre on the design with tiny stab stitches. Follow the placement guide. Repeat for petal 2. Align the outer edges of the petals with those on the design, overlapping them in the centre. Repeat for the remaining petals, layering and overlapping until all the petals are anchored to the design. Do the same for poppy 2 working from petal 1 to 5, layering and overlapping the petals as before.

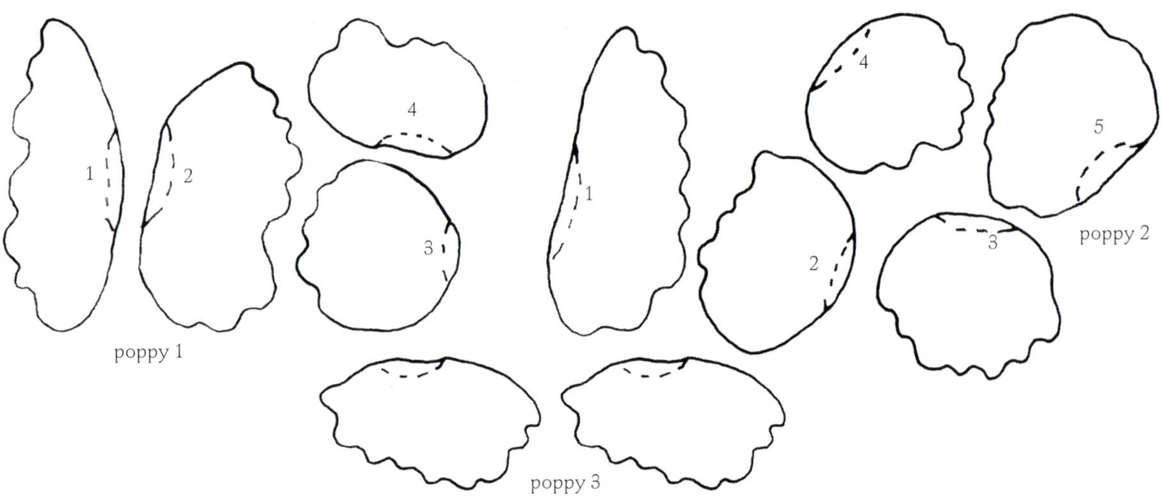

Note: *The yellow and green centres embroidered earlier and the black beads to be attached later will cover the stitches and neaten the petals.*

The petal of the open poppy no 3 on the far left is also gathered slightly and anchored like the others just beneath the yellow and green centre. Use the same Ruby Red thread and tiny stab stitches to neaten the petal of this open bud along the outer edge. Secure every centimetre or so.

Hint: *For a darker, more textured flower, lay two organza petals one on top of each other.*

Thread up with the 13-mm silk ribbon and form a few smaller petals under the organza petals of poppy 2 for an interesting texture. Lift the organza petals and use a loop stitch to form loose, looped petals. The ribbon loops will help raise the organza petals off the design for a life-like effect. Use the same ribbon and loop stitch and add a few smaller petals over the organza petals of poppy 1.

Cut out stigma no 1 along the outer dotted line. Use sharp embroidery scissors to cut a few slits on the seam of the embroidered shape.

Fold the seam to the back and attach at the back of the shape with the green thread and tiny stab stitches. Use the same green thread and tiny stab stitches to attach this shape in the centre of poppy 1. Note how the seams at the back help to pad and raise the shape. Do the same for poppy 2.

Apply Fray Stop or anti-fray agent along the edge of stigma 3 and cut along the edge of the embroidered shape. There is no seam for this shape. Attach the shape as before. Use the green silk ribbon and twisted straight stitch to form the green stem on top of the red organza petal. Lift the petals of poppy 2 and start under the petals. Insert the needle to the back just beneath the green part of the stigma.

Thread up with the black thread and attach a circle of black beads around the stigma of poppies 1 and 2. Use 3 or 4 anchoring stitches for each bead. Do the same for poppy 3 and add a few straight stitches between the beads as shown.

FINISHING THE DESIGN

Four corners

Pink flower and green leaf (top left)

CHAMELEON THREADS
Pure silk: Rose no 64, Pine Needles no 61 Use 1 strand of thread throughout
DI VAN NIEKERK'S RIBBONS
Silk 2-mm no 15; 7-mm no 43
RAJMAHAL ART SILK
No 226 Gothic Grey
STITCHES
Straight/stab stitch, detached chain/lazy daisy, ribbon stitch, pistil stitch, back stitch, satin stitch and stem stitch
NEEDLES
Use the no 9 or no 10 crewel for thread Use the no 18 chenille for the 7-mm ribbon and the no 22 or no 24 chenille for the 2-mm ribbon

Make the flower. Form the curved stem in the green thread and stem stitch, make the two leaves in the green ribbon and detached chain/lazy daisy. Thread up with the pink ribbon and form the four pink petals in ribbon stitch. Work from the centre outwards. Change to the pink thread and use tiny stab stitches along the edge of the ribbon petals to re-shape and stabilize. Change to the grey thread and use pistil stitch to form the three grey stamens in the centre of the flower.

Work the green leaf. Use the green thread and outline the leaf in back or stem stitch. Fill in the leaf in satin stitch working from the middle vein outwards. Embroider the stem and vein in stem stitch.

Blue flower and ladybird (top right)

REQUIREMENTS
Mill Hill beads no 42041
CHAMELEON THREADS
Pure silk: Forest Green no 32, Peacock no 103 Use 1 strand of thread
DI VAN NIEKERK'S RIBBONS
Silk 13-mm no 123
STITCHES
Straight/stab stitch, loop stitch, stem or split stitch, back stitch, satin stitch.
NEEDLES
Use the 9 or no 10 crewel for one strand of thread and beading Use the no 18 chenille needle for the 13-mm silk ribbon

Form the tiny stem in stem stitch using the green thread. Use the blue ribbon and make one loop stitch for each petal. Work over a large tapestry needle or similar object and only move the needle once the second stitch is made. Thread up with the blue thread and use tiny stab stitch at the base and along the edge of each loop to flatten the loops and to shape the petals. Add six or seven beads in the centre. Use the blue thread and three or four anchoring stitches for each bead.

For the ladybird, follow the instructions on page 121, using red thread instead of green or yellow.

Ant (bottom left)

Follow the instructions for the ants on page 109.

Daisy (bottom right)

Follow the instructions for the felicia on page 58.

Trapunto

The term trapunto *comes from the Italian verb* trapungere *meaning* to embroider. *It is a form of padded quilting where a shape is first outlined with rows of stitches through layers of fabric. The back layer is then cut open and padded to form a raised pattern. I have used the trapunto technique in this book to pad each panel. It is surprisingly easy to do and highly recommended if the background fabric has creases (wrinkles) once the embroidery is completed.*

Note: *If you do not wish to raise each panel, complete your sampler as detailed on* *page 146.*

REQUIREMENTS
60 x 60 cm white sheeting, polycotton, polysilk, or cotton Small, sharp pair of scissors or quick-unpick (seam ripper) Polyester toy filling or shredded batting/wadding
CHAMELEON THREADS
Pure silk: Peacock no 103 Use 2 strands of thread
STITCHES
Back or stem stitch
NEEDLES
Use the no 8 or no 9 crewel for two strands of thread

Remove your work from the hoop once the embroidery has been completed. Cut a block of white sheeting, polycotton, polysilk, or cotton similar in weight to the embroidered cloth. Too flexible a fabric, muslin for instance, results in the raised work showing more at the back than the front, which defeats the purpose. The block must be the same size as the embroidered cloth.

Lie this block of fabric flat on a table. Centre the embroidered design on top, place all the layers back in the hoop, pulling all the layers as taut as a drum (especially the back layer) tighten the hoop and roll and pin the corners out of the way.

Thread up with 2 strands of the Pacock thread and use tiny back or stem stitches along the edges of the blue border until the entire shape is encircled and you are back where you started. Take care to stitch a straight line by inserting the needle exactly on the line each time.

Still working on the hoop, turn your work to the wrong side and see how the panel is outlined at the back.

Use small, sharp scissors or a 'quick unpick' and very carefully cut a slit at the back of the work.

Hint: *Insert just the point of the scissors and lift the back fabric off the stitches before cutting further.*

Be careful not to cut the stitches. The slit is about 5 cm or 2 inches in length in the centre of the shape (just long enough to use your fingers to push the wadding into the shape, or to insert it with a hair clip or small nail file). The best padding to use is polyester toy filling or shredded batting or wadding. Insert small pieces of filling at a time, right up to the edge of the shape.

Hint: *Be careful not to over stuff. Trapunto should be a subtle enhancement where it is not noticeable at first glance.*

Position the wadding evenly-as soon as the background fabric starts to pucker, it is too full.

Take the design out of the hoop; lay the work flat on a table and check to see whether you are happy with the raised sections.

If too thick, take some filling out, if not noticeable enough – add some wadding, and if you don't like the padded section at all, remove the wadding entirely.

Close the gap with cross stitch or slip stitch.

Completing the picture

To add the finishing touches the edges of the blue border around each panel are enhanced with Peacock silk thread.

Hint: *If you don't like the Peacock thread, choose any complimentary colour used in the design. The dusty, more antique shades are good as these won't dominate or overpower the embroidered shapes in the panel. Each panel in this book was padded or raised to add an interesting finish. If you would like to do this, see page 145 and do so before following these instructions.*

CHAMELEON THREADS
Pure silk: Peacock no 103 Use 2 strands of thread
STITCHES
Back or stem stitch
NEEDLES
Use the no 8 or no 9 crewel for two strands of thread

Ensure that your design is stretched tautly in the hoop. Gently pull the fabric taut along the edges and corners and tighten the hoop all the way.

Using a no 8 or no 9 crewel needle and two strands of thread, make tiny back or stem stitches along the inside edge of the blue border until the entire shape is surrounded by stitches and you are back where you started. Take care to stitch a straight row by inserting the needle exactly on the line each time. Do the same for the outer edge of the blue border.

The outside edge of each panel is formed with the same thread and stitch to complete the picture.

Framing your picture

Choosing the mounts and frame is not an easy task for most of us. This is where a reputable framer who is experienced in framing embroideries can be a great help. Mounts and frames need to complement the picture. Because of the depth of the design, you will need to have the glass raised so that none of the features are squashed.

Bear in mind that a heavy ornate frame may overpower your picture, but a rustic wooden frame may not do it justice either.

Hint: *As you work is sure to become a treasured heirloom, it is a good idea to sign and date your work before framing it. Use a fine, sharp pencil to draw your name somewhere on the design (practise first, as you cannot rub pencil out). Cover the line with 1 strand of complementary grey or green stem and straight stitch, or use a fabric permanent marking pen, and sign your name (practise first!) Don't make your signature or date too large, as it must not be the main feature in the design. Rather have it almost hidden somewhere inbetween the leaves and flowers in the foreground. If you prefer not to sign your embroidery, why not sign and date it on the back of the framed picture?*

Application in other crafts

Various elements in panels 1 to 17 are also suitable as embellishments for the following crafts. The line drawings once enlarged, are suitable for painting on silk or fabric and can be embellished with beads and threads once painted.

CRAFT \ PANEL	1	2	3	4	5	6	7	8	9	10	11	12	13	14	15	16	17
Scrapbook pages									●					●			
Embellishing cross-stitch designs			●		●				●	●	●			●	●		●
Linen and guest towels									●						●	●	●
Machine embroidery							●	●	●	●				●	●	●	
Silk painting			●					●		●							
Card-making									●						●		
Adorning teddy bears			●	●	●				●	●	●		●	●	●	●	●
Quilt making																	
Dressmaking								●	●					●	●		
Handbags																	
Fabric painting																	
Knitted projects					●										●		
Crazy patchwork									●					●	●		
Tissue box and basket covers					●				●				●	●			
Trinket boxes or footstools																	
Cushion making			●														
Curtains and tie-backs									●				●				
Wall hangings																	
Wedding dresses			●		●			●	●	●	●		●	●	●	●	
Doll making			●		●			●	●	●			●	●	●	●	●
Candle wicking					●			●	●	●		●	●		●	●	

LEUCOSPERMUM CORDIFOLIUM
SUNBIRD
HONEYSUCKLE
TULBAGHIA
STRELITZIA
BUTTERFLY
DRAGONFLY
RESTIA
CLIVIA
CAMELLIA
FELICIA
EUCALYPTIFOLIUM
CHAMELEON
BLUE PHLOX
PENSTEMON
ROSE
BEE
BUTTERFLY
ERICA
WOOD POPPY
PIMPERNEL
BLUEBELL
SESSILE

SUNFLOWER
POPPY
PROTEA COMPACTA
MOUSE
FREESIA
Verde 2005

Enlarge image to 40,5 x 28,7 cm or 15,94 x 11,30 inches (approximately 200%)

Enlarge image to 40,5 x 28,7 cm or 15,94 x 11,30 inches (approximately 200%)

Stitch gallery

Back stitch

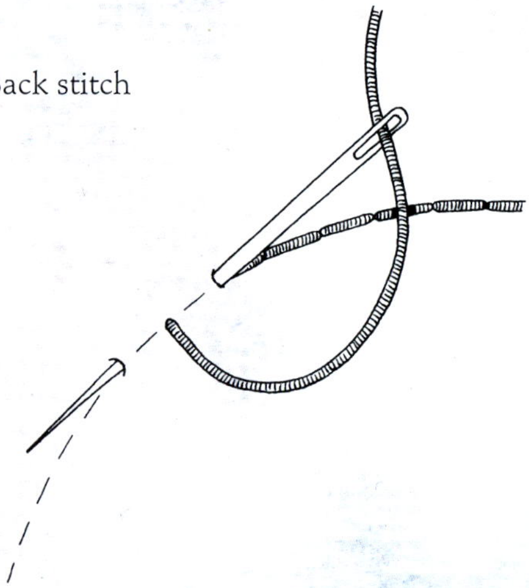

Blanket/buttonhole stitch

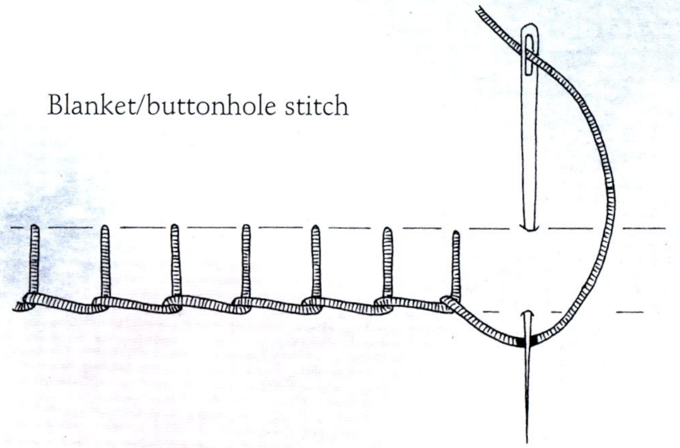

Blanket/buttonhole – detached

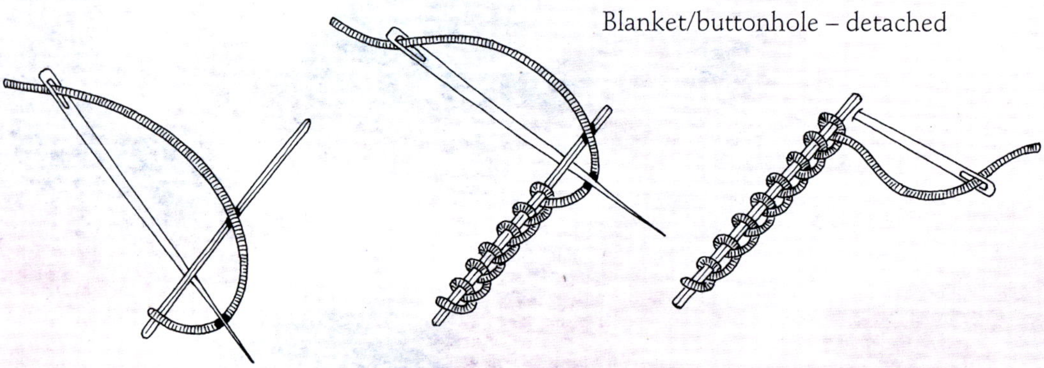

Bullion knot

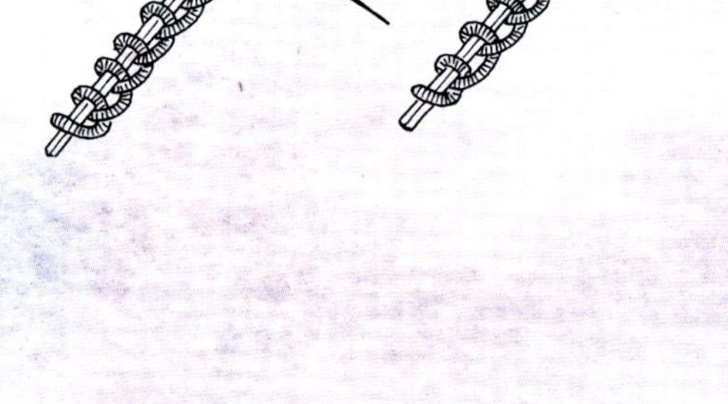

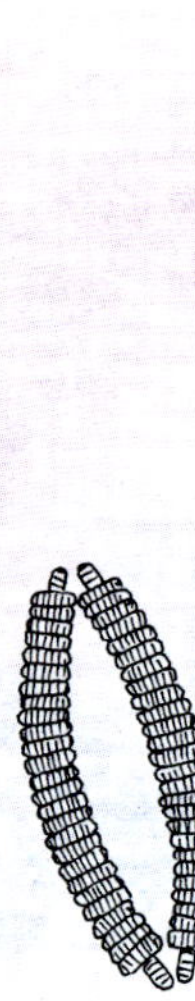

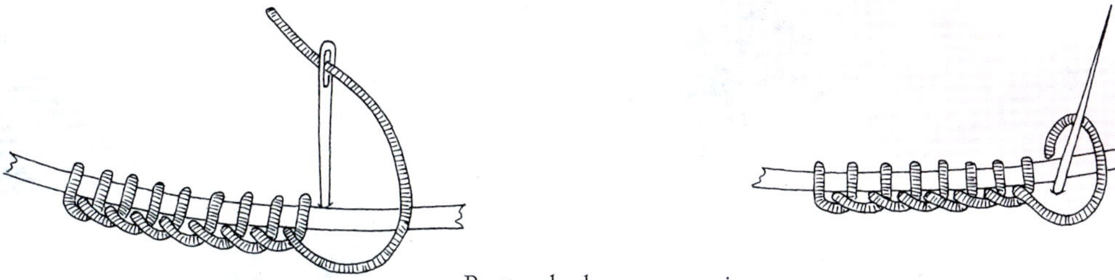

Buttonhole over a wire

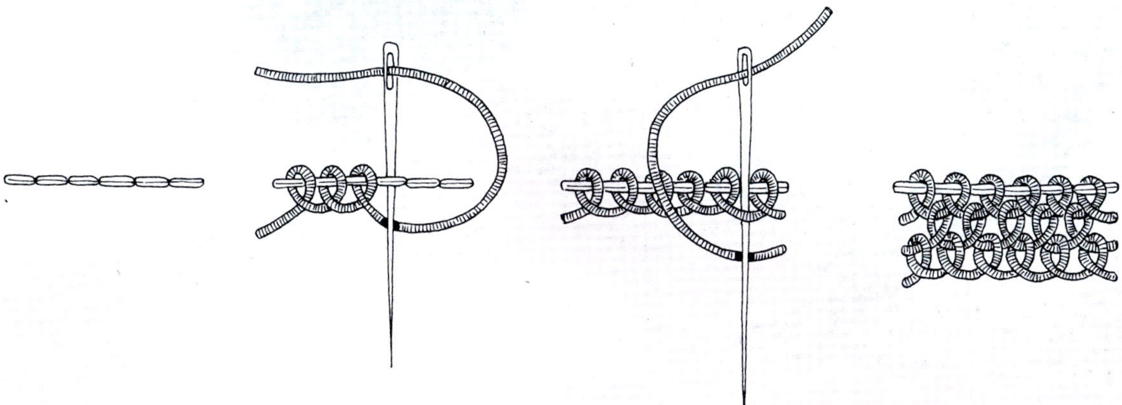

Buttonhole – open stitch

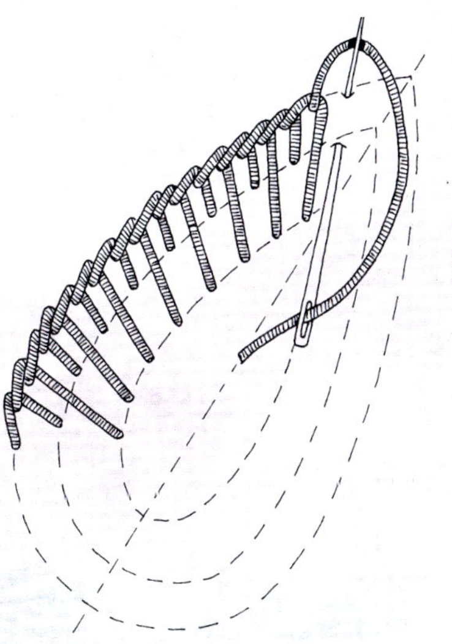

Buttonhole – long and short stitch

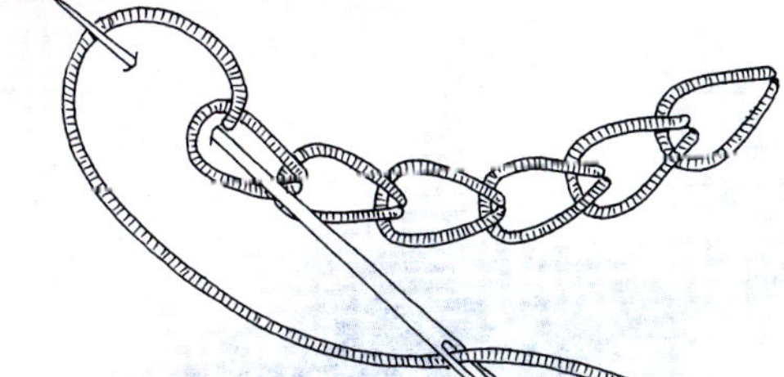

Chain stitch

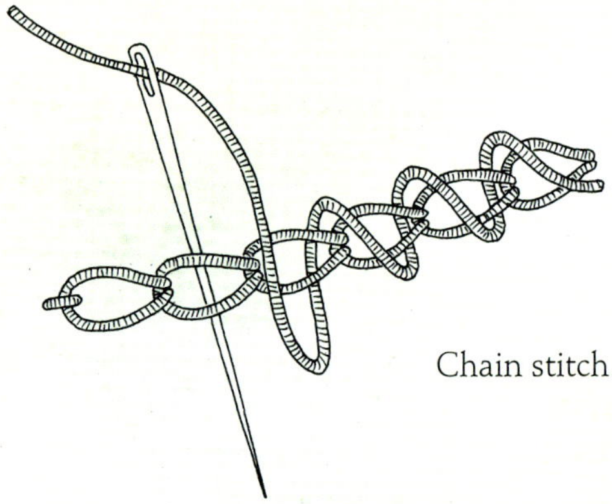

Chain stitch – whipped

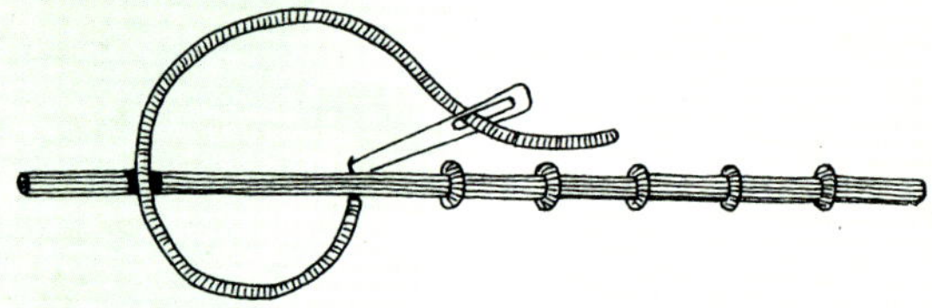

Couching

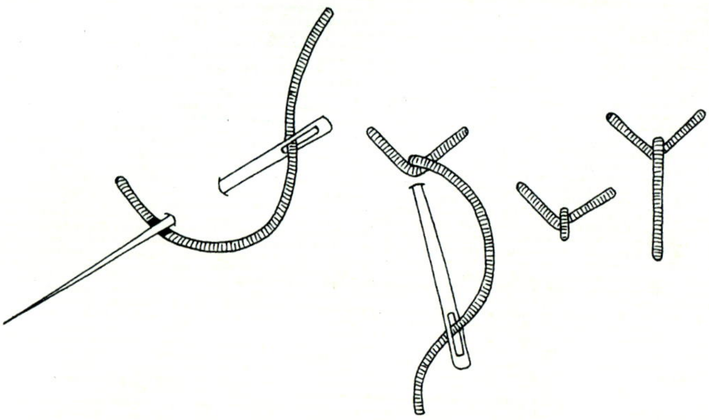

Fly stitch

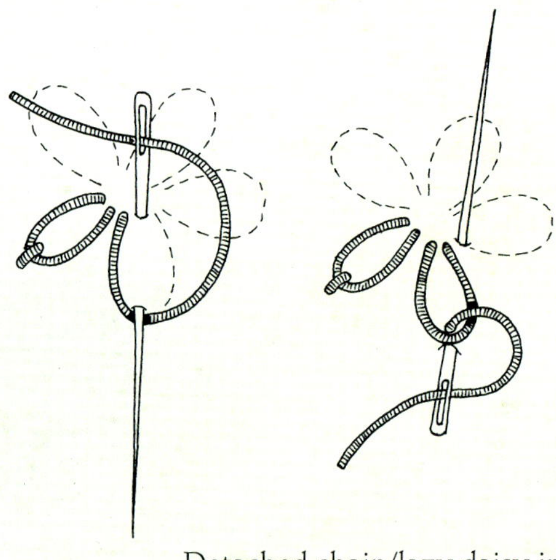

Detached chain/lazy daisy in thread

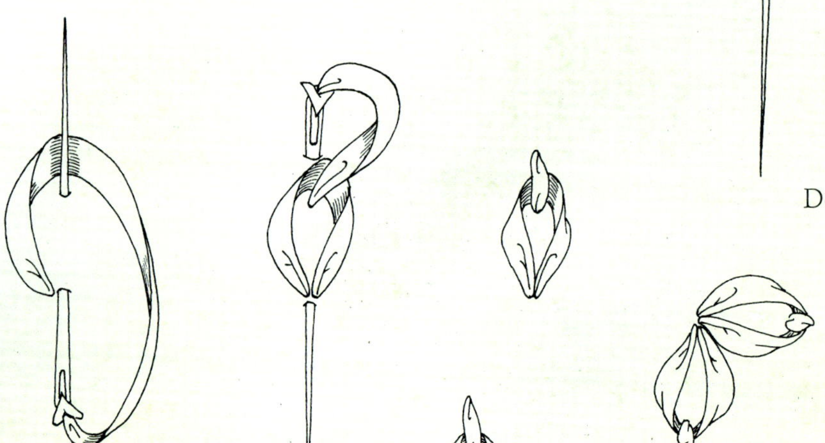

Detached chain/lazy daisy in ribbon

Long and short stitch

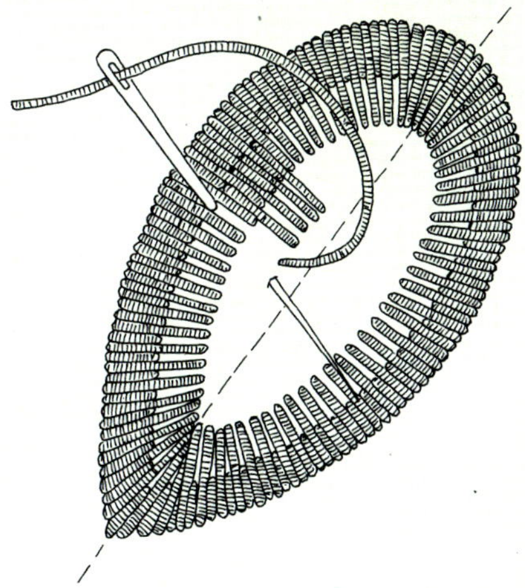

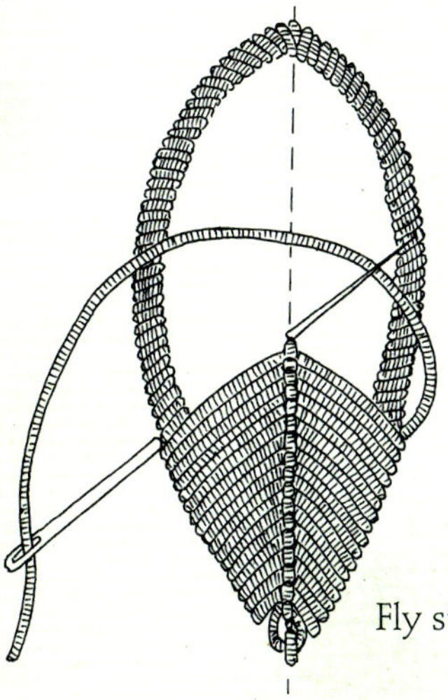

Fly stitch – padded

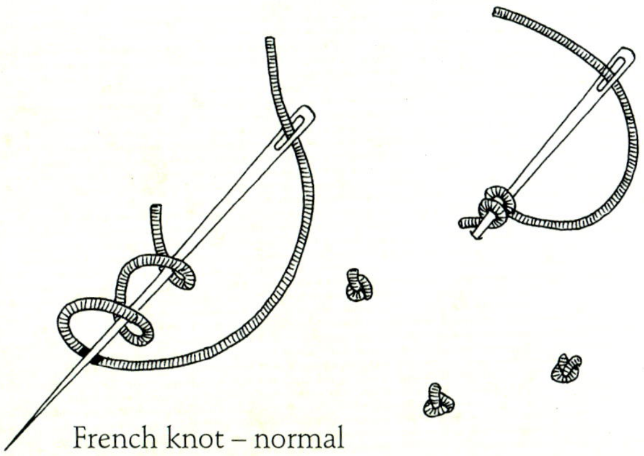

French knot – normal

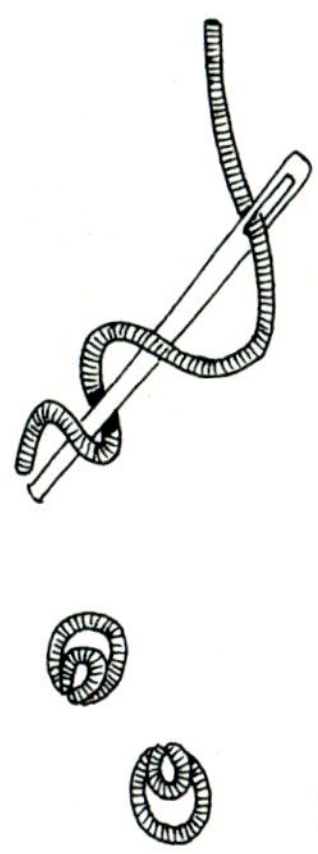

French knot – loose

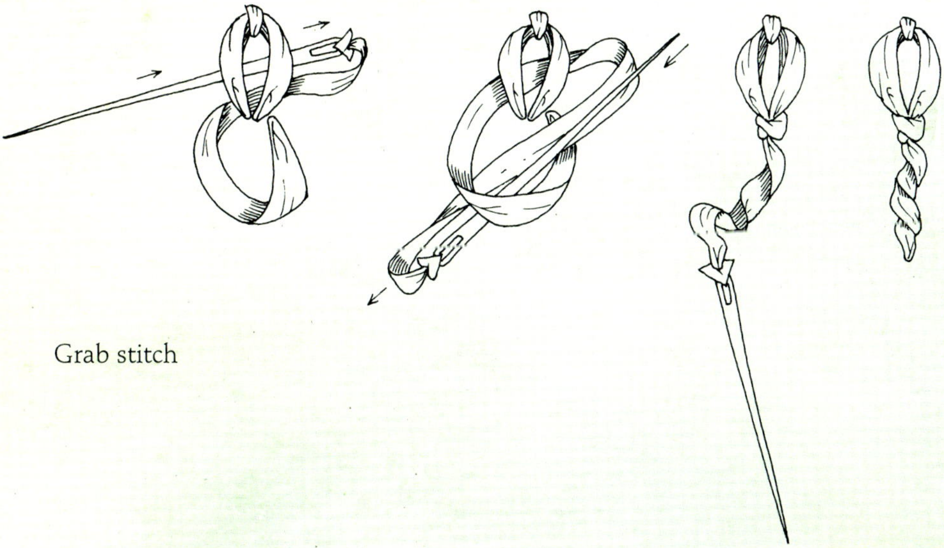

Grab stitch

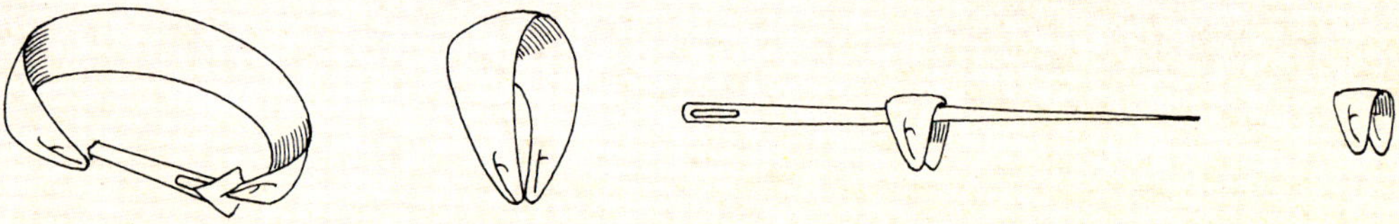

Loop stitch in ribbon

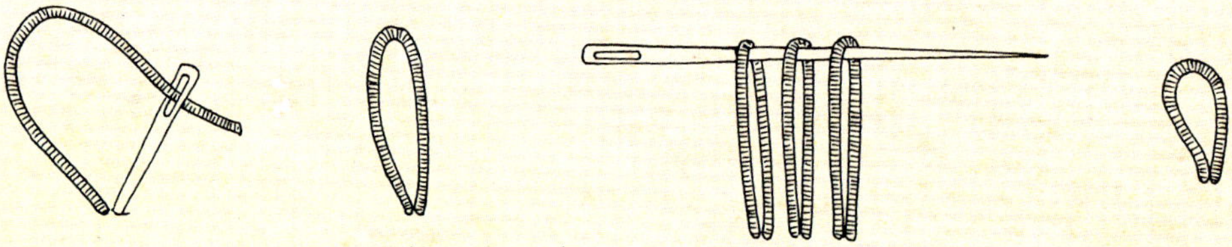

Loop stitch in thread

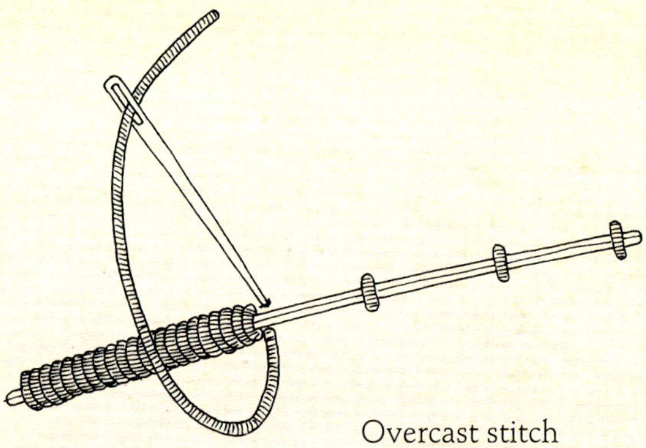

Overcast stitch

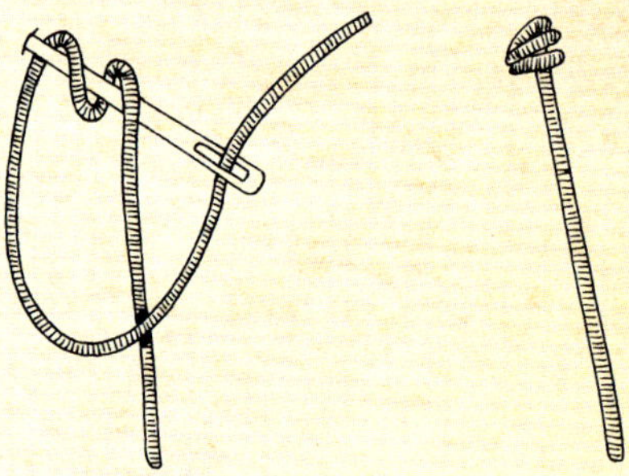

Pistil stitch

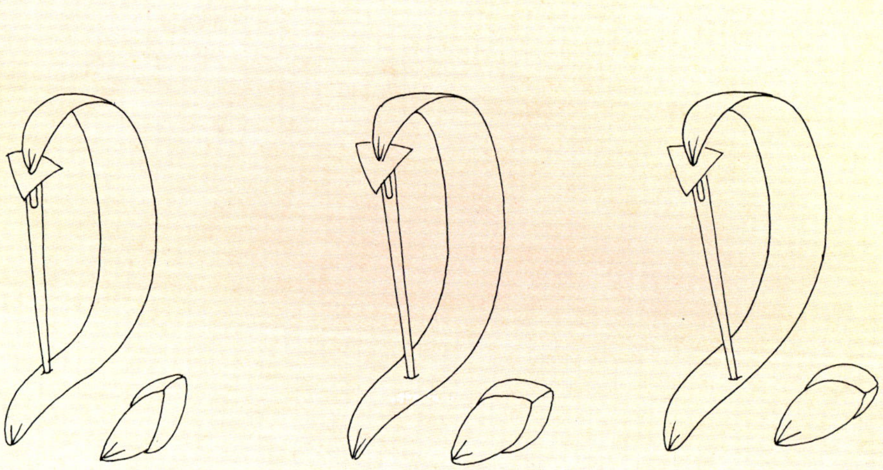

Ribbon stitch

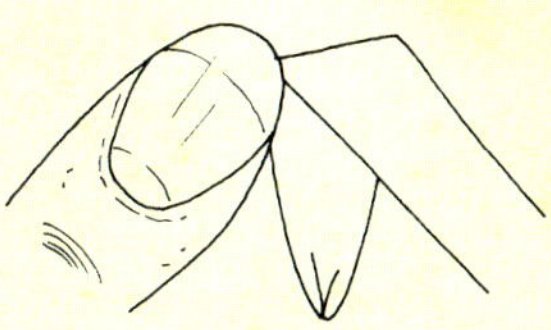

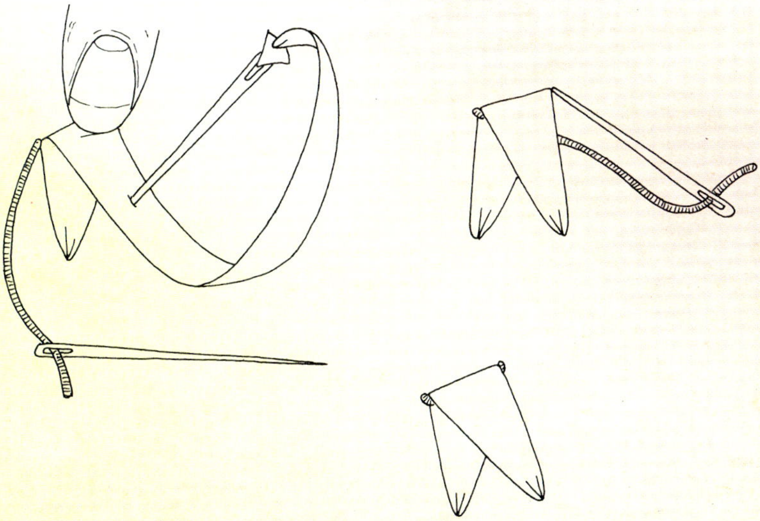

Ribbon stitch – folded

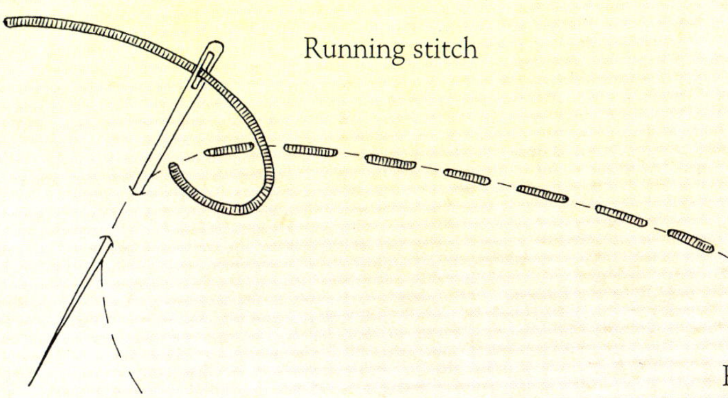

Running stitch

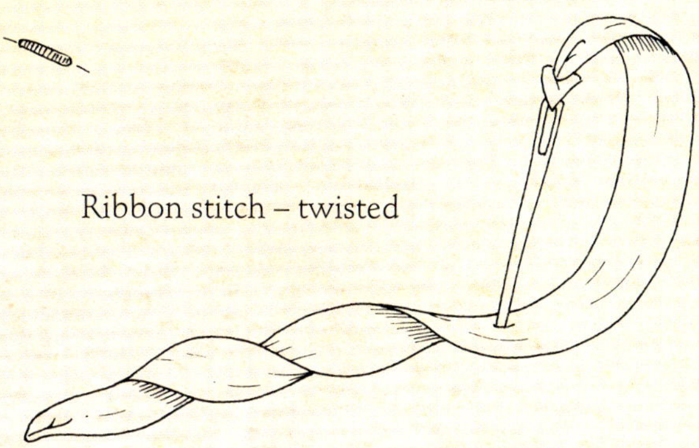

Ribbon stitch – twisted

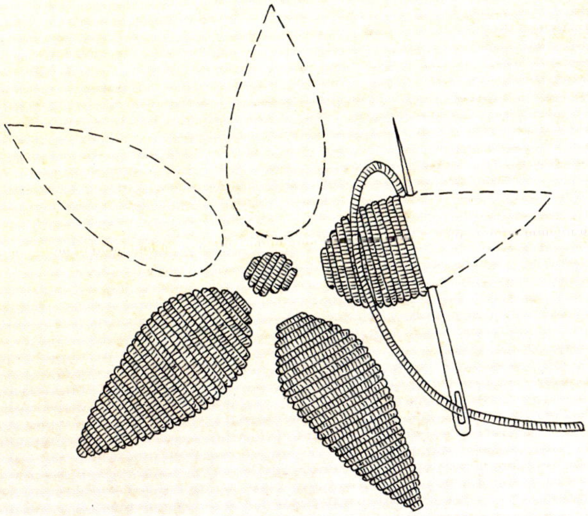

Satin stitch

Satin stitch – padded

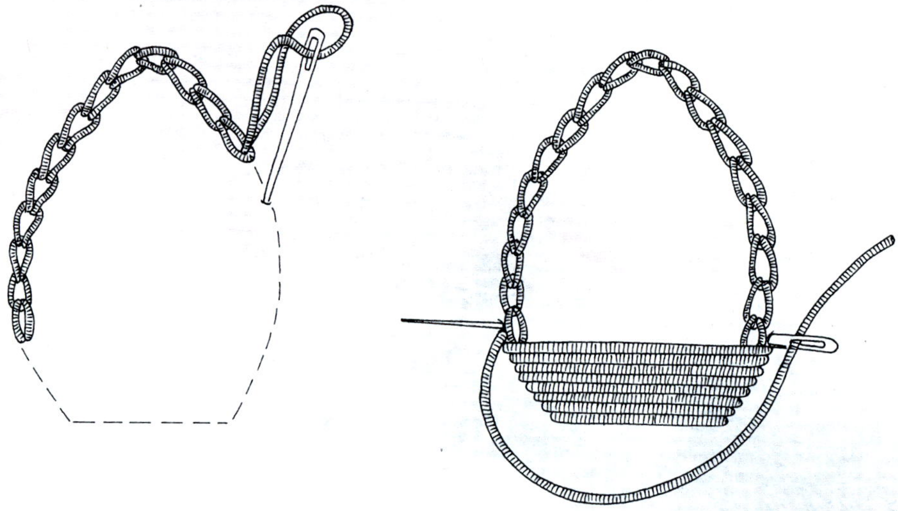

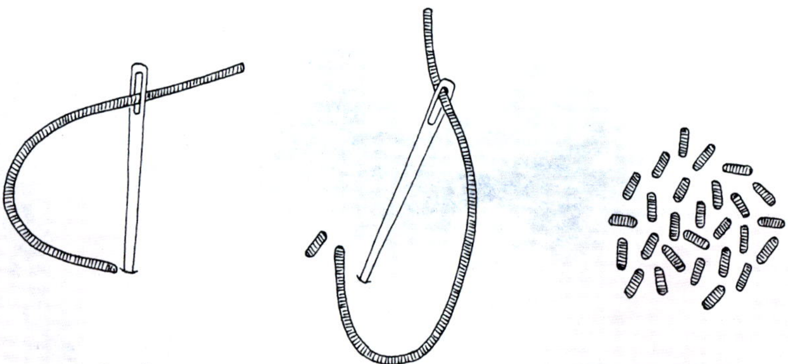

Seeding

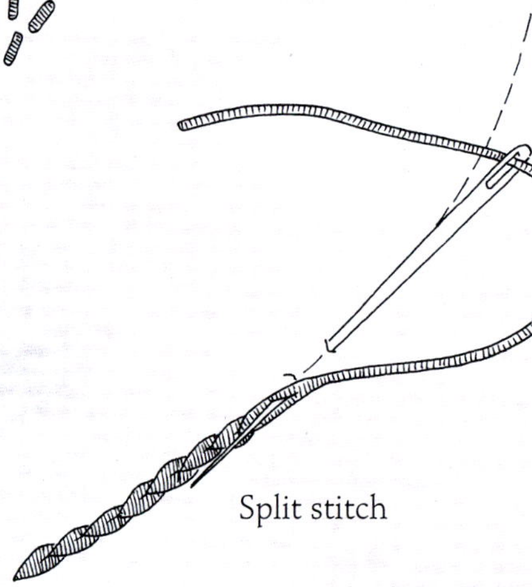

Split stitch

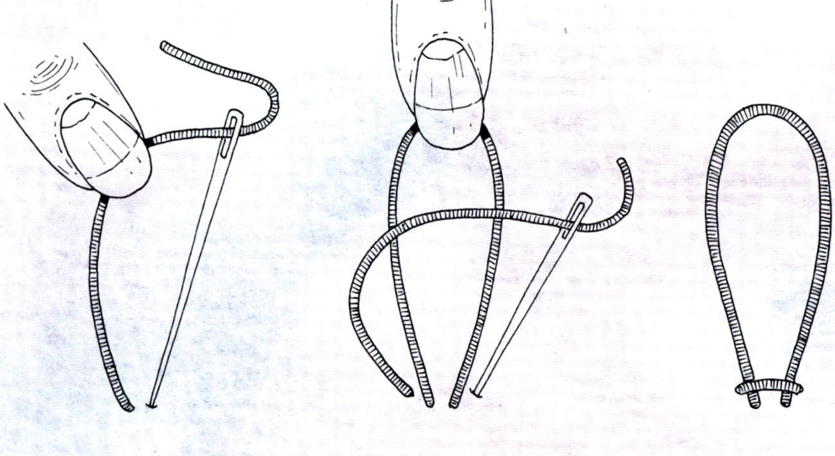

Single knotted stitch

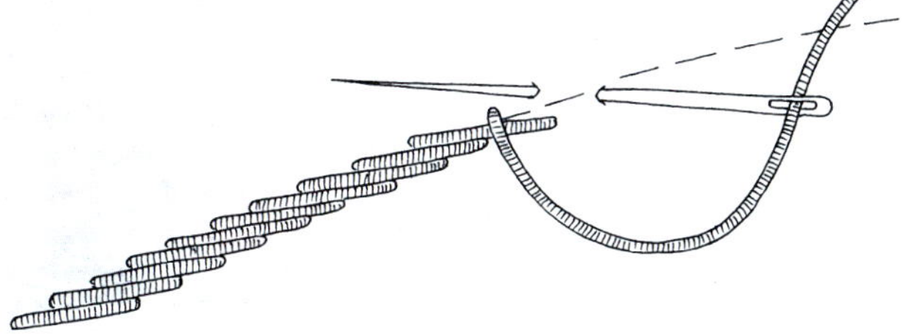

Stem stitch – traditional

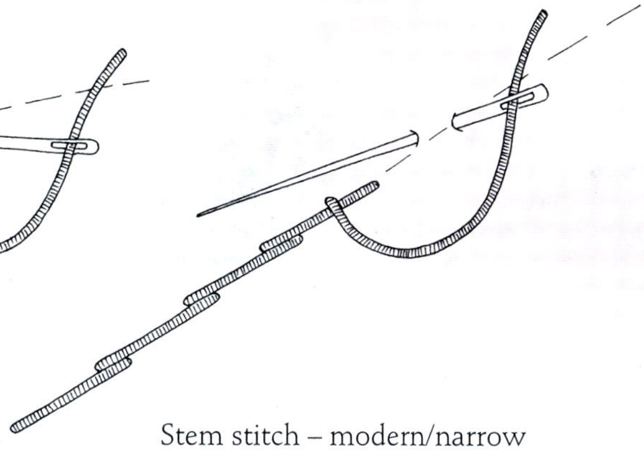

Stem stitch – modern/narrow

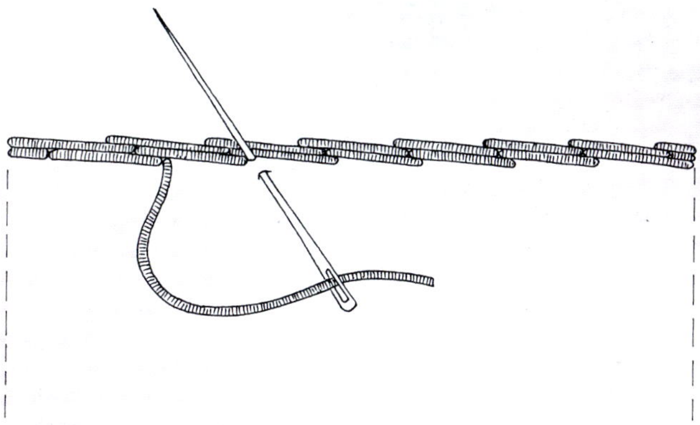

Stem stitch filling

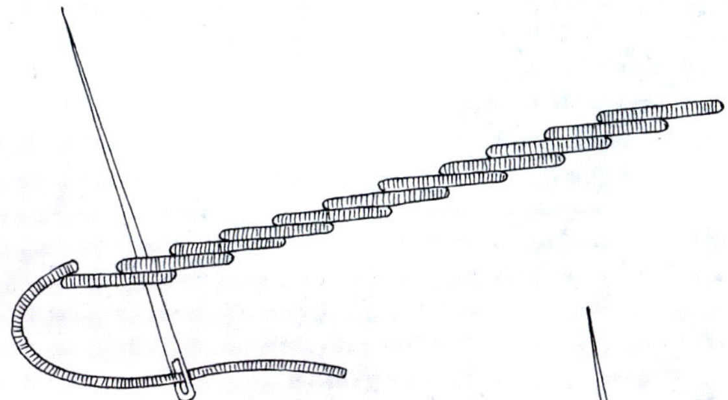

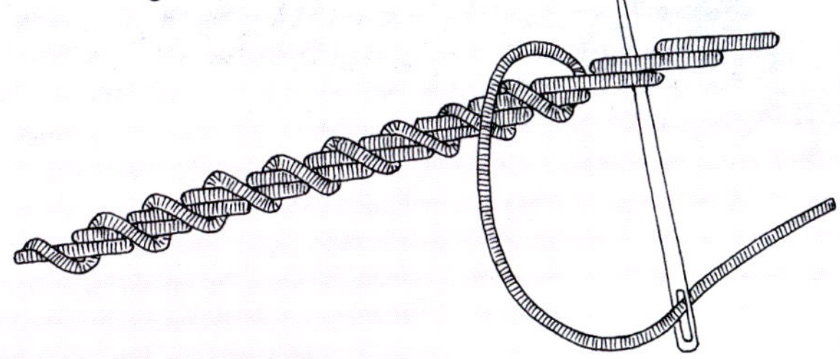

Stem stitch – whipped

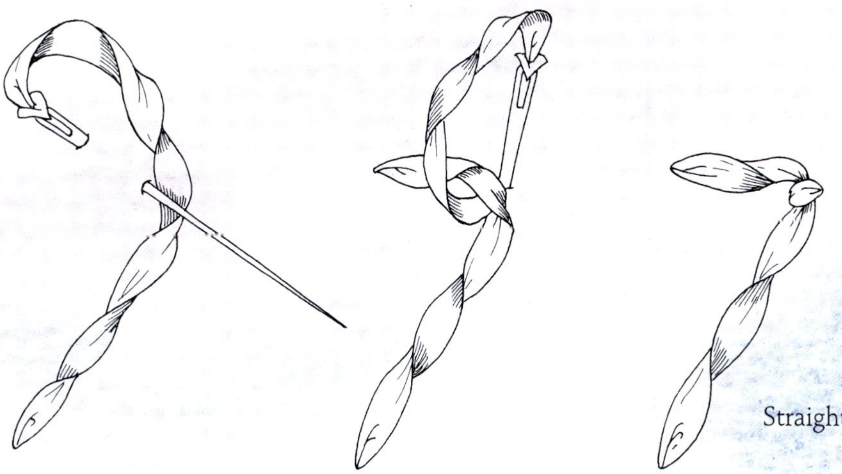

Straight stitch – folded

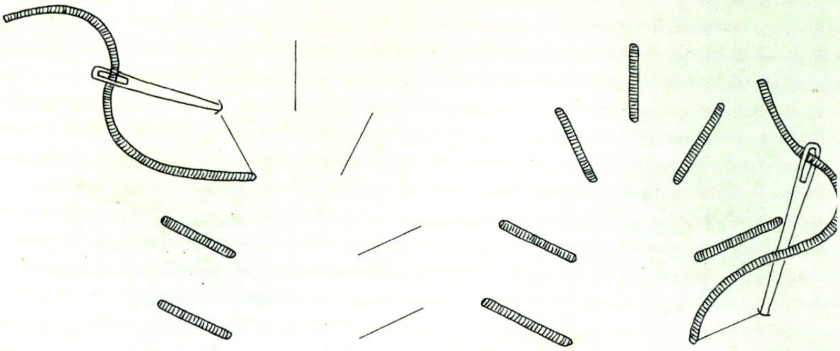

Straight/stab stitch

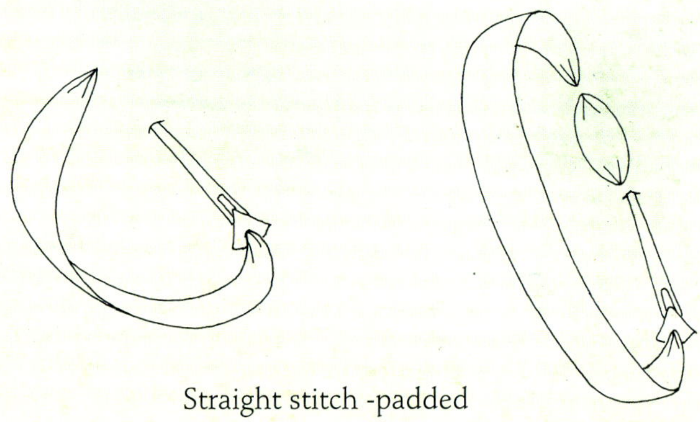

Straight stitch -padded

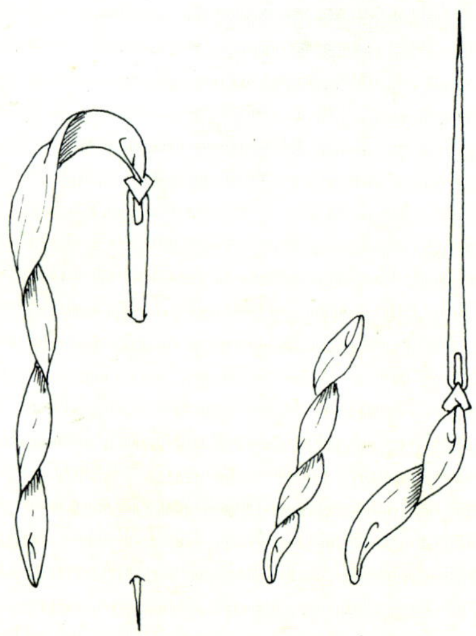

Straight stitch -twisted

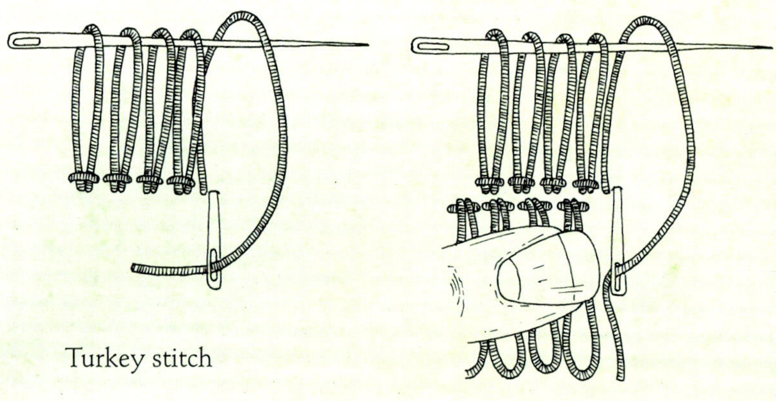

Turkey stitch

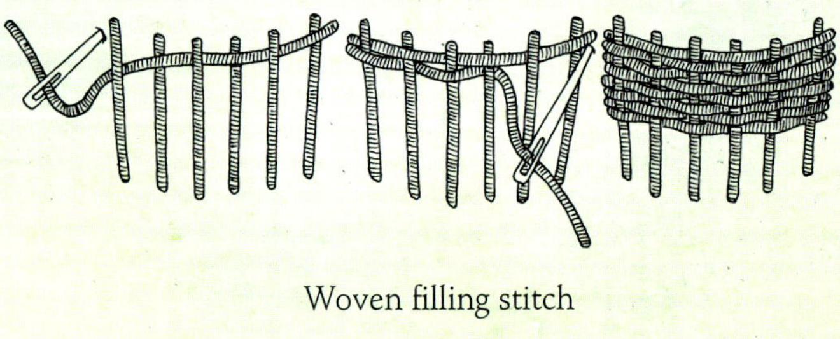

Woven filling stitch